THE NAIVE AND THE SENTIMENTAL NOVELIST

The Charles Eliot Norton Lectures • 2009

THE NAIVE AND THE SENTIMENTAL NOVELIST

ORHAN PAMUK

TRANSLATED BY NAZIM DIKBAŞ

Harvard University Press

Cambridge, Massachusetts, and London, England

2010

Library of Congress Cataloging-in-Publication Data

Pamuk, Orhan, 1952–
The naive and the sentimental novelist / Orhan Pamuk.
p. cm. —(The Charles Eliot Norton lectures)
Includes index.
ISBN 978-0-674-05076-1 (alk. paper)
1. Pamuk, Orhan, 1952–   2. Authors, Turkish—20th century—Biography.
3. Fiction—History and criticism.   4. Fiction—Technique.
5. Turkish literature.   I. Title.

PL248.P34Z46 2010
894′.3533—dc22   2010014761

To Kiran Desai

Contents

1

What Our Minds Do
When We Read Novels

Novels are second lives. Like the dreams that the French poet Gérard de Nerval speaks of, novels reveal the colors and complexities of our lives and are full of people, faces, and objects we feel we recognize. Just as in dreams, when we read novels we are sometimes so powerfully struck by the extraordinary nature of the things we encounter that we forget where we are and envision ourselves in the midst of the imaginary events and people we are witnessing. At such times, we feel that the fictional world we encounter and enjoy is more real than the real world itself. That these second lives can appear more real to us than reality often means that we substitute novels for reality, or at least that we confuse them with real life. But we never complain of this illusion, this naïveté. On the contrary, just as in some dreams, we want the novel we are reading to continue and hope that this second life will keep evoking in us a consistent sense of reality and authenticity. In spite of what we know about fiction, we are annoyed and bothered if a novel fails to sustain the illusion that it is actually real life.

We dream assuming dreams to be real; such is the definition of dreams. And so we read novels assuming them to be real—but somewhere in our mind we also know very well that our assumption is false. This paradox stems from the nature of the novel. Let us begin by emphasizing that the art of the novel relies on our ability to believe simultaneously in contradictory states.

I have been reading novels for forty years. I know there are many stances we can adopt toward the novel, many ways in which we commit our soul and mind to it, treating it lightly or seriously. And in just the same manner, I have learned by experience that there are many ways to read a novel. We read sometimes logically, sometimes with our eyes, sometimes with our imagination, sometimes with a small part of our mind, sometimes the way we want to, sometimes the way the book wants us to, and sometimes with every fiber of our being. There was a time in my youth when I completely dedicated myself to novels, reading them intently—even ecstatically. During those years, from the age of eighteen to the age of thirty (1970 to 1982), I wanted to describe what went on in my head and in my soul the way a painter depicts with precision and clarity a vivid, complicated, animated landscape filled with mountains, plains, rocks, woods, and rivers.

What takes place in our mind, in our soul, when we

read a novel? How do such interior sensations differ from what we feel when we watch a film, look at a painting, or listen to a poem, even an epic poem? A novel can, from time to time, provide the same pleasures that a biography, a film, a poem, a painting, or a fairy tale provides. Yet the true, unique effect of this art is fundamentally different from that of other literary genres, film, and painting. And I can perhaps begin to show this difference by telling you about the things I used to do and the complex images awakened within me while I was passionately reading novels in my youth.

Just like the museum visitor who first and foremost wants the painting he's gazing at to entertain his sense of sight, I used to prefer action, conflict, and richness in landscape. I enjoyed the feeling of both secretly observing an individual's private life and exploring the dark corners of the general vista. But I don't wish to give you the impression that the picture I held within me was always a turbulent one. When I read novels in my youth, sometimes a broad, deep, peaceful landscape would appear within me. And sometimes the lights would go out, black and white would sharpen and then separate, and the shadows would stir. Sometimes I would marvel at the feeling that the whole world was made of a quite different light. And sometimes twilight

would pervade and cover everything, the whole universe would become a single emotion and a single style,
and I would understand that I enjoyed this and would
sense that I was reading the book for this particular atmosphere. As I was slowly drawn into the world within
the novel, I would realize that the shadows of the actions I had performed before opening the pages of the
novel, sitting in my family's house in Beşiktaş in Istanbul—the glass of water I had drunk, the conversation
I'd had with my mother, the thoughts which had passed
through my mind, the small resentments I had har-
bored—were slowly fading away.

I would feel that the orange armchair I was sitting in,
the stinking ashtray beside me, the carpeted room, the
children playing soccer in the street yelling at each
other, and the ferry whistles from afar were receding
from my mind; and that a new world was revealing itself, word by word, sentence by sentence, in front of
me. As I read page after page, this new world would
crystallize and become clearer, just like those secret
drawings which slowly appear when a reagent is poured
on them; and lines, shadows, events, and protagonists
would come into focus. During these opening moments, everything that delayed my entry into the world
of the novel and that impeded my remembering and
envisioning the characters, events, and objects would

distress and annoy me. A distant relative whose degree
of kinship to the real protagonist I had forgotten, the
uncertain location of a drawer containing a gun, or a
conversation which I understood to have a double
meaning but whose second meaning I could not make
out—these sorts of things would disturb me enor-
mously. And while my eyes eagerly scanned the words, I
wished, with a blend of impatience and pleasure, that
everything would fall promptly into place. At such moments, all the doors of my perception would open as
wide as possible, like the senses of a timid animal re-
leased into a completely alien environment, and my
mind would begin to function much faster, almost in a
state of panic. As I focused my full attention on the details of the novel I held in my hands, so as to attune
myself to the world I was entering, I would struggle to
visualize the words in my imagination and to envision
everything described in the book.

A little later, the intense and tiring effort would yield
results and the broad landscape I wanted to see would
open up before me, like a huge continent appearing in
all its vividness after the fog lifts. Then I could see the
things recounted in the novel, like someone gazing easily and comfortably out a window and watching the
view. Reading Tolstoy's description of how Pierre
watches the Battle of Borodino from a hilltop, in *War*

and Peace, is for me like a model for reading a novel. Many details that we sense the novel is delicately weaving together and preparing for us, and that we feel the need to have available in our memory while we read, seem to appear in this scene as if in a painting. The reader gets the impression he is not among the words of a novel but standing before a landscape painting. Here, the writer's attention to visual detail, and the reader's ability to transform words into a large landscape painting through visualization, are decisive. We also read novels that do not take place in broad landscapes, on battlefields, or in nature but that are set in rooms, in suffocating interior atmospheres—Kafka's *Metamorphosis* is a good example. And we read such stories just as if we were observing a landscape and, by transforming it in our mind's eye into a painting, accustoming ourselves to the atmosphere of the scene, letting ourselves be influenced by it, and in fact constantly searching for it.

Let me give another example, again from Tolstoy, which deals with the act of gazing out a window and shows how one can enter the landscape of a novel while reading. The scene is from the greatest novel of all time, *Anna Karenina*. Anna has happened to meet Vronsky in Moscow. Returning home at night by train to St. Petersburg, she is happy because she will see

her child and her husband the next morning. I quote
from the translation by Richard Pevear and Larissa
Volokhonsky:

> Anna . . . took a paper-knife and an English novel from
> her handbag. At first she was unable to read. To begin
> with, she was bothered by the bustle and movement;
> then, when the train started moving, she could not
> help listening to the noises; then the snow that beat
> against the left-hand window and stuck to the glass,
> and the sight of a conductor passing by, all bundled up
> and covered with snow on one side, and the talk about
> the terrible blizzard outside, distracted her attention.
> Further on, it was all the same: the same jolting and
> knocking, the same snow on the window; the same
> quick transitions from steaming heat to cold and back
> to heat, the same flashing of the same faces in the
> semi-darkness, and the same voices, and Anna began
> to read and understand what she was reading. Anna
> Arkadyevna read and understood, but it was unpleas-
> ant for her to read, that is, to follow the reflection of
> other people's lives. She wanted too much to live her-
> self. When she read about the heroine of the novel tak-
> ing care of a sick man, she wanted to walk with inaudi-
> ble steps round the sick man's room; when she read
> about a Member of Parliament making a speech, she

wanted to make that speech; when she read about how Lady Mary rode to hounds, teasing her sister-in-law and surprising everyone with her courage, she wanted to do it herself. But there was nothing to do, and so, fingering the smooth knife with her small hands, she forced herself to read.

Anna is unable to read because she cannot help thinking of Vronsky, because she wants to live. If she were able to focus on her novel, she could easily imagine Lady Mary mounting her horse and following the pack of hounds. She would visualize the scene as if she were gazing out a window and would feel herself slowly entering this scene she observes from the outside.

Most novelists sense that reading the opening pages of a novel is akin to entering a landscape painting. Let us remember how Stendhal begins *The Red and the Black*. We first see from afar the town of Verrières, the hill it is situated on, the white houses with their peaked red-tile roofs, the clumps of flourishing chestnut trees, and the ruins of the town's fortifications. The River Doubs flows below. Then we notice the sawmills and the factory that produces *toiles peintes*, colorful printed textiles.

Only a page later we have already met the mayor, one of the central characters, and have identified his cast of mind. The real pleasure of reading a novel starts with the ability to see the world not from the outside but through the eyes of the protagonists living in that world. When we read a novel, we oscillate between the long view and fleeting moments, general thoughts and specific events, at a speed which no other literary genre can offer. As we gaze at a landscape painting from afar, we suddenly find ourselves among the thoughts of the individual in the landscape and the nuances of the person's mood. This is similar to the way we view a small human figure depicted against crags, rivers, and myriad-leaved trees in Chinese landscape paintings: we focus on him, and then try to imagine the surrounding landscape through his eyes. (Chinese paintings are designed to be read in this manner.) Then we realize that the landscape has been composed to reflect the thoughts, emotions, and perceptions of the figure within it. Likewise, as we sense that the landscape within the novel is an extension of, a part of, the mental state of the novel's protagonists, we realize that we identify with these protagonists via a seamless transition. Reading a novel means that, while committing the overall context to memory, we follow, one by one, the thoughts and actions of the protagonists and ascribe meaning to them within the general landscape. We are now inside the landscape that a short while ago we were gazing at from the outside: in addition to seeing the mountains in our mind's eye, we feel the coolness of the river and catch the scent of the forest, speak to the protagonists and make our way deeper into the universe of the novel. Its language helps us to combine these distant and distinct elements, and see both the faces and the thoughts of the protagonists as part of a single vision.

Our mind works hard when we are immersed in a novel, but not like Anna's mind as she sits in the noisy, snow-covered St. Petersburg train. We continually oscillate between the landscape, the trees, the protagonists, the protagonists' thoughts, and the objects they touch—from the objects to the memories they evoke, to the other protagonists, and then to general thoughts. Our mind and our perception work intently, with great rapidity and concentration, carrying out numerous operations simultaneously, but many of us no longer even realize that we are carrying out these operations. We are exactly like someone driving a car, who is unaware that he is pushing knobs, depressing pedals, turning the wheel carefully and in accordance with many rules, reading and interpreting road signs, and checking the traffic while he drives.

The analogy of the driver is valid not only for the reader but also for the novelist. Some novelists are unaware of the techniques they are using; they write spontaneously, as if they were carrying out a perfectly natural act, oblivious to the operations and calculations they are performing in their head and to the fact that they are using the gears, brakes, and knobs that the art of the novel equips them with. Let us use the word "naive" to describe this type of sensibility, this type of novelist and novel reader—those who are not at all concerned with the artificial aspects of writing and reading a novel. And let us use the term "reflective" to describe precisely the opposite sensibility: in other words, the readers and writers who are fascinated by the artificiality of the text and its failure to attain reality, and who pay close attention to the methods used in writing novels and to the way our mind works as we read. Being a novelist is the art of being both naive and reflective at the same time.

Or being both naive and "sentimental." Friedrich Schiller was the first to propose this distinction, in his famous essay "Über naive und sentimentalische Dichtung" (On Naive and Sentimental Poetry; 1795–1796). The word *sentimentalisch* in German, used by Schiller to describe the thoughtful, troubled modern poet who has lost his childlike character and naïveté, is somewhat different in meaning from the word "sentimental," its counterpart in English. But let us not dwell on this word, which, in any case, Schiller borrowed from English, inspired by Laurence Sterne's *Sentimental Journey*. (Listing examples of naive, childlike geniuses, Schiller respectfully mentions Sterne, along with others such as Dante, Shakespeare, Cervantes, Goethe, and even Dürer.) It suffices for us to note that Schiller uses the word *sentimentalisch* to describe the state of mind which has strayed from nature's simplicity and power and has become too caught up in its own emotions and thoughts. My aim here is to reach a deeper understanding of Schiller's essay, which I have loved very much since my youth, as well as to clarify my own thoughts on the art of the novel via his essay (as I have always done) and to express them accurately (as I am striving to do now).

In that famous work, described by Thomas Mann as the "most beautiful essay in the German language," Schiller divides poets into two groups: the naive and the sentimental. Naive poets are one with nature; in fact, they are like nature—calm, cruel, and wise. They write poetry spontaneously, almost without thinking, not bothering to consider the intellectual or ethical consequences of their words and paying no attention to what others might say. For them—in contrast to contemporary writers—poetry is like an impression that nature makes upon them quite organically and that never leaves them. Poetry comes spontaneously to naive poets from the natural universe they are part of. The belief that a poem is not something thought out and deliberately crafted by the poet, composed in a certain meter and shaped via constant revision and self-criticism, but rather something that should be written unreflectively and that may even be dictated by nature or God or some other power—this Romantic notion was advocated by Coleridge, a devoted follower of the German Romantics, and was clearly expressed in the 1816 preface to his poem "Kubla Khan." (Ka, the poet protagonist of my novel *Snow,* wrote his poems under the Coleridge-Schiller influence and with the same naive view of poetry.) In Schiller's essay, which evokes great admiration in me every time I read it, there is one attribute among the defining characteristics of the naive poet that I wish to emphasize in particular: the naive poet has no doubt that his utterances, words, verse will portray the general landscape, that they will represent it, that they will adequately and thoroughly describe and reveal the meaning of the world—since this meaning is neither distant nor concealed from him.

By contrast, according to Schiller, the "sentimental" (emotional, reflective) poet is uneasy, above all, in one respect: he is unsure whether his words will encompass reality, whether they will attain it, whether his utterances will convey the meaning he intends. So he is exceedingly aware of the poem he writes, the methods and techniques he uses, and the artifice involved in his endeavor. The naive poet does not differentiate much between his perception of the world and the world itself. But the modern, sentimental-reflective poet questions everything he perceives, even his very senses. And he is concerned about educative, ethical, and intellectual principles when he casts his perceptions into verse.

Schiller's famous and I think very amusing essay is an attractive source for those who want to contemplate the interrelation of art, literature, and life. I read it over and over again in my youth, thinking about the examples it presented, the types of poets it spoke of, and the differences between writing spontaneously and writing in a deliberate and self-aware way aided by the intellect. As I read the essay, I also of course thought about myself as a novelist and the various moods I experienced when writing novels. And I recalled what I had felt when working on my paintings a few years earlier. From the age of seven until I was twenty-two, I constantly painted with the dream of someday becoming a painter, but I had remained a naive artist and had abandoned painting, perhaps after becoming aware of this. Back then, as well, I thought of what Schiller called "poetry" as being art and literature in the most general sense. I will do the same during these talks, in keeping with the spirit and tradition of the Norton Lectures. This dense and provocative work by Schiller will accompany me while I contemplate the art of the novel, reminding me along the way of my own youth, which discreetly oscillated between the "naive" and the "sentimental."

Actually, beyond a certain point Schiller's essay is no longer only about poetry, or about art and literature in general, but becomes a philosophical text on human types. At this point, where the text reaches its dramatic and philosophical peak, I enjoy reading the personal thoughts and opinions between the lines. When Schiller says, "There are two different types of humanity," he also wants to say, according to German literary historians, "Those that are naive like Goethe and those that are sentimental like me!" Schiller envied Goethe not only for his poetic gifts, but also for his serenity, unaffectedness, egoism, self-confidence, and aristocratic spirit; for the way he effortlessly came up with great and brilliant thoughts; for his ability to be himself; for his simplicity, modesty, and genius; and for his unawareness of all this, precisely in the manner of a child. In contrast, Schiller himself was far more reflective and intellectual, more complex and tormented in his literary activity, far more aware of his literary methods, full of questions and uncertainties regarding them—and felt that these attitudes and traits were more "modern."

While reading "On Naive and Sentimental Poetry" thirty years ago, I too—just like Schiller raging at Goethe—complained of the naive, childlike nature of Turkish novelists of the previous generation. They wrote their novels so easily, and never worried about problems of style and technique. And I applied the word "naive" (which I increasingly used in a negative sense) not only to them but to writers all over the world who regarded the nineteenth-century Balzacian novel as a natural entity and accepted it without question. Now, after an adventure of thirty-five years as a novelist, I would like to continue with my own examples, even as I try to convince myself that I have found an equilibrium between the naive novelist and the sentimental novelist inside me.

Earlier, when discussing the world depicted in novels, I used the analogy of the landscape. I added that some of us are oblivious to what our mind does when we read novels, like motorists who are unaware of the operations they perform when driving a car. The naive novelist and the naive reader are like people who sincerely believe that they understand the country and the people they see from the window as the car moves through the landscape. And since this type of person believes in the power of the landscape he can see from his car window, he may begin to talk about the people and make pronouncements which evoke envy in the sentimental-reflective novelist. In contrast, the sentimental-reflective novelist will say that the view from the car window is limited by the frame and that the windshield is muddy anyway, and he will withdraw into a Beckettian silence. Or, like me and many other contemporary literary novelists, he will depict the wheel, the knobs, the muddy window, and the gears as part of the scene, so we never forget that what we see is restricted by the novel's point of view.

Before we are swept away by analogy and seduced by Schiller's essay, let us carefully list the most important actions that take place in our mind when we read a novel. Reading a novel always entails these operations, but only novelists of a "sentimental" spirit can recognize them and come up with a detailed inventory. Such a list will remind us of what the novel actually is— something we know, but may well have forgotten. Here are the operations our mind performs when we read a novel:

1. We observe the general scene and follow the narrative. In the book he wrote on Cervantes' *Don Quixote*, Spanish thinker and philosopher José Ortega y Gasset says that we read adventure novels, chivalric novels,

cheap novels (detective novels, romance novels, spy novels, and so on may be added to this list) to see what happens next; but we read the modern novel (he meant what we today call the "literary novel") for its atmosphere. According to Ortega y Gasset, the atmosphere novel is something more valuable. It's like a "landscape painting," and contains very little narrative.

But we read a novel—whether it has a lot of narrative and action, or no narrative at all, like a landscape painting—always in the same fundamental manner. Our usual practice is to follow the narrative and try to figure out the meaning and main idea that are suggested by the things we encounter. Even if a novel, just like a landscape painting, depicts many individual tree-leaves one by one without narrating a single event (the sort of technique used in, say, a French *nouveau roman* by Alain Robbe-Grillet or Michel Butor), we begin to consider what the narrator is trying to imply in this way, and what kind of story these leaves will eventually form. Our mind constantly searches for motive, idea, purpose, a secret center.

2. We transform words into images in our mind. The novel tells a story, but the novel is not only a story. The story slowly emerges out of many objects, descriptions, sounds, conversations, fantasies, memories, bits of information, thoughts, events, scenes, and moments. To

derive pleasure from a novel is to enjoy the act of departing from words and transforming these things into images in our mind. As we picture in our imagination what the words are telling us (what they want to tell us), we readers complete the story. In doing this, we propel our imagination by searching for what the book says or what the narrator wants to say, what he intends to say, what we guess he is saying—in other words, by searching for the novel's center.

3. Another part of our mind wonders how much of the story the writer tells is real experience and how much is imagination. We ask this question especially in the parts of the novel that arouse our wonder, admiration, and amazement. To read a novel is to wonder constantly, even at moments when we lose ourselves most deeply in the book: How much of this is fantasy, and how much is real? A logical paradox exists between, on the one hand, the experience of losing oneself in the novel and naively thinking it is real, and, on the other, one's sentimental-reflective curiosity about the extent of fantasy it contains. But the inexhaustible power and vitality of the art of the novel stem from its unique logic and from its reliance on this type of conflict. Reading a novel means understanding the world via a non-Cartesian logic. By this I mean the constant and steadfast ability to believe simultaneously in contradic-

tory ideas. Thus, a third dimension of reality slowly begins to emerge within us: the dimension of the complex world of the novel. Its elements conflict with one another, yet at the same time are accepted and described.

4. Still we wonder: Is reality like this? Do the things narrated, seen, and described in the novel conform with what we know from our own lives? For instance, we ask ourselves: Could a passenger on the night train from Moscow to St. Petersburg in the 1870s easily find enough comfort and quiet to read a novel, or is the writer trying to tell us that Anna is a genuine booklover who likes to read even amid noisy distractions? At the heart of the novelist's craft lies an optimism which thinks that the knowledge we gather from our everyday experience, if given proper form, can become valuable knowledge about reality.

5. Under the influence of such optimism, we both assess and derive pleasure from the precision of analogies, the power of fantasy and narrative, the buildup of sentences, the secret and candid poetry and music of prose. Problems and pleasures of style are not at the heart of the novel, but they are somewhere very close to it. Yet this inviting topic can be approached only via thousands of examples.

6. We make moral judgments about both the choices and the behavior of the protagonists; at the same time,

we judge the writer for his moral judgments regarding his characters. Moral judgment is an unavoidable quagmire in the novel. Let us always keep in mind that the art of the novel yields its finest results not through judging people but through understanding them, and let us avoid being ruled by the judgmental part of our mind. When we read a novel, morality should be a part of the landscape, not something that emanates from within us and targets the characters.

7. As our mind performs all of these operations simultaneously, we congratulate ourselves on the knowledge, depth, and understanding we have attained. Especially in novels of high literary quality, the intense relationship we establish with the text seems to us readers to be our own private success. The sweet illusion that the novel was written solely for us slowly arises within us. The intimacy and confidence that develop between the writer and ourselves help us to evade, and to avoid worrying too much about, the parts of the book we cannot understand, or things we oppose or find unacceptable. In this way, we always enter into complicity with the novelist to a certain extent. As we read a novel, one part of our mind is busy concealing, conniving, shaping, and constructing positive attributes that foster this complicity. In order to believe the narrative, we choose not to believe the narrator as much as

he wants us to—because we want to continue faithfully reading the narrative, despite finding fault with some of the writer's opinions, propensities, and obsessions.

8. While all this mental activity is going on, our memory is laboring intensely and incessantly. In order to find meaning and readerly pleasure in the universe the writer reveals to us, we feel we must search for the novel's secret center, and we therefore try to embed every detail of the novel in our memory, as if learning each leaf of a tree by heart. Unless the writer has simplified and diluted his world so as to help the inattentive reader, remembering everything is a difficult task. This difficulty also defines the boundaries of novelistic form. The novel must be of a length that allows us to remember all the details we've gathered in the process of reading, because the meaning of everything we encounter as we move through the landscape is related to everything else we have come across. In well-constructed novels, everything is connected to everything else, and this entire web of relations both forms the atmosphere of the book and points toward its secret center.

9. We search for the novel's secret center with utmost attention. This is the most frequent operation our mind performs when we read a novel, whether naively unaware or sentimentally reflective. What sets novels apart

from other literary narratives is that they have a secret center. Or, more precisely, they rely on our conviction that there is a center we should search for as we read.

What is the novel's center made of? Everything that makes the novel, I could reply. But we are somehow convinced that this center is far from the novel's surface, which we pursue word by word. We imagine it is somewhere in the background, invisible, difficult to trace, elusive, almost dynamic. We optimistically think that the indicators of this center are everywhere and that the center connects all the details in the novel, everything we encounter on the surface of the broad landscape. In my lectures I will discuss how real and how imaginary this center is.

Because we know—or assume—that novels have centers, we act, as readers, exactly like the hunter who treats each leaf and each broken branch as a sign and examines them closely as he progresses through the landscape. We move forward sensing that each new word, object, character, protagonist, conversation, description, and detail, all of the linguistic and stylistic qualities of the novel and the twists of its narrative, imply and point to something other than what is immediately apparent. This conviction that the novel has a center makes us feel that a detail we assume to be irrelevant might be significant, and that the meaning of everything on the surface of the novel might be quite different. Novels are narratives open to feelings of guilt, paranoia, and anxiety. The sense of depth which we feel when we read a novel, the illusion that the book immerses us in a three-dimensional universe, stems from the presence of the center, whether real or imaginary.

The primary thing that separates a novel from an epic poem, a medieval romance, or a traditional adventure narrative is this idea of a center. Novels present characters that are much more complex than those in epics; they focus on everyday people and delve into all the aspects of everyday life. But they owe these qualities and powers to the presence of a center somewhere in the background, and to the fact that we read them with this kind of hope. As the novel reveals to us life's mundane details and our small fantasies, daily habits, and familiar objects, we read on curiously—in fact, in amazement—because we know they indicate a deeper meaning, a purpose somewhere in the background. Every feature of the general landscape, each leaf and flower, is interesting and intriguing because there is meaning hidden behind it.

Novels can address people of the modern era, indeed all humanity, because they are three-dimensional fictions. They can speak of personal experience, the knowledge we acquire through our senses, and at the same time they can provide a fragment of knowledge, an intuition, a clue about the deepest thing—in other words, the center, or what Tolstoy would call the meaning of life (or however we refer to it), that difficult-to-reach place we optimistically think exists. The dream of attaining the deepest, dearest knowledge of the world and of life without having to endure the difficulties of philosophy or the social pressures of religion—and doing this on the basis of our own experience, using our own intellect—is a very egalitarian, very democratic kind of hope.

It was with great intensity and this particular hope that I read novels between the ages of eighteen and thirty. Every novel I read, sitting transfixed in my room in Istanbul, offered me a universe as rich in life-detail as any encyclopedia or museum, as richly human as my own existence, and full of demands, consolations, and promises which in depth and scope were comparable only to those found in philosophy and religion. I read novels as if in a dream state, forgetting everything else, in order to gain knowledge of the world, to construct myself, and to shape my soul.

E. M. Forster, who will appear from time to time during these lectures, says in *Aspects of the Novel* that "the final test of a novel will be our affection for it." The value of a novel, for me, lies in its power to provoke a search for a center which we can also naively project upon the world. To simplify: the real measure of that value must be the novel's power to evoke the sense that life is indeed exactly like this. Novels must address our main ideas about life, and must be read with the expectation that they will do so.

Because of their structure, suited to the pursuit and discovery of a hidden meaning or a lost value, the most suitable genre for the spirit and form of the novelistic art is what the Germans call the *Bildungsroman,* or "novel of formation," which tells of the shaping, education, and maturation of young protagonists as they become acquainted with the world. In my youth, I trained myself by reading such books (Flaubert's *Sentimental Education,* Mann's *Magic Mountain*). Gradually I began to see the fundamental knowledge that the center of the novel presented—knowledge about what kind of place the world was, and about the nature of life, not only in the center but everywhere in the novel. This was perhaps because each sentence of a good novel evokes in us a sense of the profound, essential knowledge of what it means to exist in this world, and the nature of that sense. I also learned that our journey in this world, the life we spend in cities, streets, houses, rooms, and nature, consists of nothing but a search for a secret meaning which may or may not exist.

In these talks, we will investigate how the novel can bear all this weight. Just like readers searching for the center as they read a novel, or naive young protagonists in a *Bildungsroman* searching for the meaning of life with curiosity, sincerity, and faith, we will try to progress toward the center of the art of the novel. The broad landscape we move through will take us to the writer, to the idea of fiction and fictionality, to characters in novels, to the narrative plot, to the problem of time, to objects, to seeing, to museums, and to places we cannot yet anticipate—perhaps just like a real novel.

2

Mr. Pamuk, Did All This Really Happen To You?

Nurturing a love of novels, developing the habit of reading novels, indicates a desire to escape the logic of the single-centered Cartesian world where body and mind, logic and imagination, are placed in opposition. Novels are unique structures that allow us to keep contradictory thoughts in our mind without uneasiness, and to understand differing points of view simultaneously. I touched upon this in my previous lecture.

I would now like to reveal to you two of my beliefs, which are firm and strong, as well as contradictory. But first allow me to set the context. In 2008, I published in Turkey a novel entitled *The Museum of Innocence*. This novel is concerned with (among other things) the actions and feelings of a man called Kemal, who is deeply and obsessively in love. It wasn't long before I began receiving the following question from a number of readers, who apparently thought that his love was described in a highly realistic manner: "Mr. Pamuk, did all this actually happen to you? Mr. Pamuk, are you Kemal?"

So now let me give my two contradictory answers, both of which I believe sincerely:

1. "No, I am not my hero Kemal."
2. "But it would be impossible for me to ever convince readers of my novel that I am not Kemal."

The second answer suggests that it would be difficult for me—as it so often is for novelists—to convince my readers that they should not equate me with my protagonist; at the same time, it implies that I do not intend to exert a great deal of effort to prove I am not Kemal. In fact, I wrote my novel knowing very well that my readers—we could refer to them as naive, unassuming readers—would think that Kemal was me. Besides, somewhere in the back of my mind, part of me *wanted* my readers to think I was Kemal. In other words, I intended my novel to be perceived as a work of fiction, as a product of the imagination—yet I also wanted readers to assume that the main characters and the story were true. And I did not feel at all like a hypocrite or a trickster for harboring such contradictory desires. I have learned through experience that the art of writing a novel is to feel these contradictory desires deeply, but to peacefully continue writing, unperturbed.

When Daniel Defoe published *Robinson Crusoe,* he concealed the fact that the story was a fiction born of his imagination. He claimed that it was a true story, and then, when it emerged that his novel was a "lie," he became embarrassed, and admitted—though only to a certain extent—the fictionality of his story. For many hundreds of years—from *Don Quixote* or even *The Tale of Genji*, to *Robinson Crusoe, Moby-Dick,* and the literature of today—writers and readers have been trying unsuccessfully to come to some agreement on the nature of the novel's fictionality.

I wouldn't want these words to suggest that I hope such agreement will be reached. On the contrary, the art of the novel draws its power from the absence of a perfect consensus between writer and reader on the understanding of fiction. Readers and authors acknowledge and agree on the fact that novels are neither completely imaginary nor completely factual. But as we read a novel, word after word, sentence after sentence, this awareness is transformed into questioning, into a strong and focused curiosity. Clearly the writer must have experienced *something* of the sort, the reader thinks, but perhaps he has exaggerated or imagined part of it. Or on the contrary, the reader, presuming that writers are capable of writing only about what they have experienced, may begin to imagine the "truth" about the writer. Depending on their naïveté and their feelings about the book, readers may have contradictory thoughts about the blending of reality and imagination in the novel they are holding in their hands. In fact, when reading the same novel at two different times, they may have conflicting opinions regarding the extent to which the text might be true to life or, on the other hand, a figment of the imagination.

Wondering about which parts are based on real-life experience and which parts are imagined is but one of the pleasures we find in reading a novel. Another, related pleasure stems from reading what novelists say in their prefaces, on book jackets, in interviews, and in memoirs as they try to persuade us that their real-life experiences are products of their imagination or that their made-up narratives are true stories. Like many readers, I enjoy reading this "meta-literature," which sometimes takes a theoretical, metaphysical, or poetic form. The claims and justifications that novelists use to legitimize their texts, the unusual language, the disingenuousness, evasions, and inconsistencies, the borrowed forms and sources, are sometimes as revealing as the novels themselves. The impact a novel has on its readers is partly formed, as well, by what critics say about it in newspapers and magazines and by the writer's own statements aimed at controlling and manipulating the way it is received, read, and enjoyed.

In the three hundred years since Defoe, wherever the art of the novel has taken root, it has supplanted other literary genres, beginning with poetry. And it has rap-

idly become the dominant literary form, gradually dis-
seminating, in societies around the world, the concept
of fiction we agree on today (or agree to disagree on).
The film industry was built on the idea of fiction developed and spread by the novel; and in turn, in the twentieth century, it transformed this idea into something
we now all accept, or at least seem to accept. This process can be likened to the way the art of painting that
developed during the Renaissance, an art based on perspective, established a dominant position (aided by the
invention of photography and the craft of reproduction) across the entire world within the space of four
centuries. Just as the way a handful of fifteenth-century
Italian painters and aristocrats saw and depicted the
world is now accepted everywhere as the norm, replac-
ing other ways of seeing and depicting, so the idea of
fiction disseminated by the novel and popular cinema
has been accepted around the globe as a natural thing,
and the details of its historical origins have been largely
forgotten. This is where we find ourselves in the current
landscape.

We are already familiar to a certain extent with the
story of the rise of the novel in England and France,
and how the idea of fiction was established in these
countries. But we know less about the discoveries made
and the solutions found by writers who imported the

art of the novel *from* those places—in particular, how they adapted the concept of fiction recognized in the West to their own reading publics and national cultures. At the heart of these problems and the new voices and forms they engendered lies the process by which the Western idea of fictionality underwent a creative and practical adaptation to local cultures. Non-Western authors, who found themselves obliged to fight against prohibitions, taboos, and the repression of authoritarian states, used the borrowed idea of the novel's fictionality to speak about "truths" they could not openly express—just as the novel had formerly been used in the West.

When these writers said that their novels were entirely products of the imagination—a claim opposite to Defoe's, who insisted that his story was the "complete truth"—they were of course lying, just like Defoe. Yet they did this not to deceive readers, as Defoe had done, but to protect themselves from regimes that might ban their books and punish the authors. On the other hand, these same writers wanted to be understood and read in a certain way; and so in interviews, prefaces, and jacket copy, they continued to imply that their novels actually told the "truth" and were all about "reality." Eventually, in order to shake off the moral burden of their contradictory stance, which led them into hypoc-

risy, some non-Western novelists even began to develop
a sincere belief in the things they had said. The creation
of original voices and new forms of the novel, in controlled societies, came about as a result of these politi-
cally necessary reactions and maneuverings. Here I am
thinking of Mikhail Bulgakov's *The Master and Mar-
garita,* Sadegh Hedayat's *The Blind Owl,* Junichiro
Tanizaki's *Naomi,* and Ahmet Hamdi Tanpınar's *The
Time Regulation Institute* (*Saatleri Ayarlama Enstitüsü*),
which can all be read allegorically.

Non-Western novelists—wishing to emulate the high
aesthetic level that the novel had reached in, say, London or Paris, and often trying to counter the sort of
fiction widely accepted in their countries (perhaps saying, "They don't write like this in Europe anymore")
—wanted to use, adapt, and implement in their own
countries the latest forms of the novel, the latest ideas
of fiction. At the same time, they wanted to employ
fictionality as a shield against the repression of the state
(perhaps saying, "Do not accuse me—my novels are
products of the imagination"). And *at the same time,*
they wanted to boast of openly stating the truth. These
contradictory stances—which are practical solutions to
oppressive social and political conditions—give rise to
new forms and novelistic techniques, especially outside
Western cultural centers.

If we could conduct a thorough study of the way fictionality has been used by novelists in repressive non-Western societies, starting in the late 1800s and continuing throughout the twentieth century, country by country and writer by writer—a complex and highly intriguing story—we would see that creativity and originality mostly came about as a reaction to these contradictory desires and demands. Even now that the concept of fiction established by the modern novel has been accepted throughout the world, largely thanks to the cinema, the question "Did all this really happen to you?"—a relic of Defoe's time—has not lost its validity. On the contrary, for the past three hundred years this question has been one of the main forces sustaining the art of the novel and accounting for its popularity.

Since I have referred to the cinema, allow me to give an example from *The Museum of Innocence,* a novel that deals with the Turkish film industry in the 1970s. I confess, without the slightest trace of a smile, that I actually wrote scripts for Turkish films in the early 1980s and experienced first-hand some of the things I put into the novel. In the early 1970s, the Turkish film industry was thriving and attracted very large audiences. Back then, it was proudly asserted that Turkey produced more films per year than any other country in the world except the United States and India. In those films, famous actors would use their real names for their characters, and might star in roles that closely resembled the lives they actually lived. For instance, Türkan Şoray, the great celebrity of the period, would portray the famous film star Türkan Şoray in an imaginary story, and later, in the interviews she gave after the film's release, would attempt to close the gap between her real life and the life she depicted in the film. Just as credulous readers believe that the hero of a novel represents the author himself, or some other actual person, filmgoers believed unquestioningly that the Türkan Şoray on the silver screen represented the Türkan Şoray in real life—and fascinated by the differences between them, they would try to make out which details were true and which were imagined.

Whenever I read *In Search of Lost Time*, which describes the world of a man not unlike Proust, I too am curious to know which details and episodes the author actually lived, and to what extent. This is why I like biographies, and why I do not laugh at the naïveté of viewers who confuse a film star with the character she plays. Even more interesting for the purposes of this lecture, and in the context of a discussion about the art of the novel, are the attitudes of supposedly "savvy" readers. They may smile at the gullibility of film viewers and roar with laughter when semi-famous actors known for playing bad guys in films are scolded, beaten, and nearly lynched by angry viewers who recognize them on the streets of Istanbul. Still, such "sophisticated" readers cannot help asking, "Mr. Pamuk, are you Kemal? Did all this really happen to you?" Such questions are a useful reminder that novels can mean different things to different readers, from all social classes and all cultures.

Before I give a second example on this subject, let me say that I often agree with those who warn against trying to understand a novel by looking at the author's life, and against confusing a novel's hero with its writer. Not long after *The Museum of Innocence* was published in Istanbul, I ran into an old friend I hadn't seen in years, a professor with whom I discuss such matters from time to time. Thinking he would offer some sympathy, I complained that everyone was asking, "Are you Kemal, Mr. Pamuk?" We chatted about this as we walked through the streets of Nişantaşı, where my novel takes place. We recalled the passage in Book 11 of Rousseau's *Confessions*, where Rousseau complained about reactions to his novel *Julie; or The New Heloise* ("What made women so favorable to me was their being persuaded that I had written my own history and that I myself was the hero of the romance"). We re-

membered the essay "What Is an Author?" by Michel
Foucault, the concepts of the ideal reader and the im-
plied reader, and the writings of Wolfgang Iser and
Umberto Eco (the latter, who had delivered these
Norton Lectures in 1993, was an author we both admired). My gentle friend brought up the Arab poet Abu
Nuwas, whom I mention in my novel *The Black Book,*
in the chapter entitled "Three Musketeers"—a hetero-
sexual who wrote as if he were a homosexual. And he
told me that, over the centuries, many Chinese writers
had adopted female personas in their works. Like a pair
of non-Western intellectuals who are forever complaining about the lack of sophistication of their fellow
countrymen, we discussed, with no great concern, how
readers' interest in gossip was encouraged by the newspapers, and how this was preventing people in Turkey
from acquiring a Western understanding of fiction and
the novel.

Just then, my old friend stopped in front of an apart-
ment building opposite the Teşvikiye Mosque. I
stopped as well, and looked at him quizzically.

"I thought you were going home," he said.

"I am, but I don't live here," I replied.

"Really?" said the professor. "I figured from your
novel that your hero Kemal lived here with his mother."

He smiled at his mistake. "I must have unconsciously assumed that you, too, had moved here with your mother."

Like old men who have reached the point where they can take anything in stride, we smiled at each other for confusing fiction with reality. We sensed that we had fallen under this illusion not because we had forgotten that novels are based on imagination just as much as on fact, but because novels impose this illusion upon readers. And now we also began to perceive that we liked to read novels precisely for this purpose: in order to blend the imaginary with the real. What we were feeling at that moment was—in the terms I've proposed in these lectures—the desire to be both "naive" and "sentimental" at the same time. Reading a novel, just like writing one, involves a continual oscillation between these two mindsets.

I can now introduce the actual theme of this lecture: the writer's "signature"—his or her unique way of rendering the world. But let me first recall one or two things I mentioned in my first lecture. I spoke of the real or imaginary center that is located somewhere in the background of each novel and that separates novels from other detailed narratives, such as adventure accounts and epic poems. Novels take us to the secret truth they promise, to the center, by starting from the

small details and events we all observe in everyday life
and are familiar with in our own way. To simplify, let us
call each of these observations a *sensory experience.*
When we open a window, take a sip of coffee, climb a
flight of stairs, immerse ourselves in a crowd, get stuck
in a traffic jam, pinch our finger in a door, lose our
glasses, shiver in the cold, climb a hill, go swimming on
the first day of summer, meet a beautiful woman, taste
a kind of cookie we haven't eaten since childhood, sit in
a train and look out the window, smell a flower we've
never seen before, get annoyed with our parents, ex-
change a kiss, see the ocean for the first time, become
jealous, drink a glass of cold water—the uniqueness of
each of these sensations, and the way they overlap with
the experiences of other people, form the basis of our
understanding and enjoying a novel.

Reading the description of Anna Karenina trying to
read in the compartment of a night train during a
snowstorm, we remember that we have had similar sensory experiences. We too, perhaps, have traveled on a
night train through a dense snowfall. We too may have
had difficulty reading a novel when our mind was occupied with other things. Our experience probably did
not take place on the Moscow–St. Petersburg train, as
Anna's does in Tolstoy's narrative. But we have had
enough similar experiences so that we can share the

character's sensations. The universal suggestiveness and limits of novels are determined by this shared aspect of everyday life. When no one ever again travels by night train with a novel for a companion, readers will have difficulty understanding Anna's situation on the train; and when tens of thousands of such details disappear and fade, readers will have difficulty understanding *Anna Karenina* the novel.

What Anna Karenina felt on the train is so similar yet at the same time so different from our own experience that it has the ability to enchant us. Since, in a corner of our mind, we also know that these details, these sensations, can come only from life itself, by *being lived,* we know that Tolstoy is relating to us, through Anna Karenina, his own life experience and his own sensory universe. This, then, should be precisely what is meant by the much-quoted words attributed to Flaubert: "I am Madame Bovary." Flaubert was not a woman; he never married; his life bore no resemblance to that of his heroine. But he lived and witnessed her sensory experiences the way she did (her unhappiness, her yearning for a colorful life, the pettiness of small-town life in nineteenth-century France, the bitter difference between dreams and middle-class reality). He expressed his way of seeing as Madame Bovary's way of seeing, and did so in a completely convincing way. Yet despite all his talent and his powers of expression—perhaps thanks to this talent—there are times when we feel that Flaubert might have imagined all those details which seem so true to life.

The precision, clarity, and beauty of the details, the sense that "Yes, it is exactly so, there we have it," which the description evokes within us, and the inspiring ability of a text to bring a scene to life in our imagination—these are the qualities that make us admire a writer. We also feel that such a writer has a gift for expressing sensations just as if he had experienced them himself, and can persuade us he has lived things he has only imagined. Let us call this illusion the *power* of the novelist. Once again, I would like to emphasize what a wonderful thing this power is. And once again, I would like to stress that while it is perhaps temporarily possible to forget the presence of the novelist while reading a novel, we can never achieve this in a sustained way, because we are always comparing the sensory details of the narrative with our own life experience, and depicting them in our mind through that knowledge. One of the essential pleasures we find in reading novels—just as Anna Karenina does when reading on the train—is that of comparing our life with the lives of others. This is true even when we read novels that appear to be based entirely on imagination. Historical novels, fantastic novels, science fiction novels, philosophical novels, romances, and many other books that blend these various types are actually, just like so-called realist novels, based on everyday observations of life in the period in which they were written.

Once we have searched for a deeper meaning in the novel's complex landscape, have derived pleasure from the sensory experience of the protagonists (the way the world appears to the characters, as revealed in conversations and the small details of their lives), and have completely immersed ourselves in the world of the novel, we can forget about the writer himself. In fact, in one part of our mind—the part that makes us naive— we can even forget that the novel we are holding was conceived and composed by a writer. A characteristic feature of the novel is that the writer is most present in the text at the moments we most completely forget about him. This is because the times we forget about the writer are the times we believe the fictional world to be actual, to be the real world; and we believe the writer's "mirror" (this is an old-fashioned metaphor for the way the novel portrays, or "reflects," reality) to be a perfect and natural mirror. There is, of course, no such thing as a perfect mirror. There are only mirrors that perfectly meet our expectations. Every reader who decides to read a novel chooses a mirror according to his or her taste.

When I say there is no such thing as a perfect mirror, I am referring to more than mere differences in style. Something else—something that renders all literature possible—is our subject now. What we feel when we open the curtains to let the sunlight in, when we wait for an elevator that refuses to arrive, when we enter a room for the first time, when we brush our teeth, when we hear the sound of thunder, when we smile at someone we hate, when we fall asleep in the shade of a tree—our sensations are both similar to and different from those of other people. The similarities allow us to imagine the whole of mankind through literature, and also enable us to conceive of a world literature— a world novel. But each novelist has a different way of experiencing, and writing about, the coffee he drinks, the rising of the sun, and his first love. These differences extend to all of the novelist's heroes. And they form the basis of that novelist's style and signature.

"Mr. Pamuk, I have read all your books," a woman once said to me in Istanbul. She was approximately the age of my aunt, and had the air of an aunt about her. "I know you so well, you'd be surprised." Our eyes met. A feeling of guilt and embarrassment came over me, and I thought I understood what she meant. The remark of the worldly-wise lady who was almost a generation older than me, the embarrassment I felt at that moment, and the implications of her gaze stayed in my mind as the days passed, and I tried to understand what had confused me.

When this lady who reminded me of my aunt said, "I know you," she wasn't claiming that she knew my life story, my family, where I lived, the schools I'd attended, the novels I'd written, and the political difficulties I'd suffered. Nor did she know my private life, my personal habits, or my essential nature and worldview, which I had tried to convey by linking them to my native city in my book *Istanbul*. The elderly lady was not confusing my story with the stories of my fictional characters. She seemed to be talking about a deeper, more intimate, more secret thing, and I felt I understood her. What allowed the insightful aunt to know me so well were my own sensory experiences, which I had unconsciously put into all my books, all my characters. I had projected my experiences onto my characters: how I feel when I inhale the scent of rain-soaked earth, when I get drunk in a noisy restaurant, when I touch my father's false teeth after his death, when I regret that I am in love, when I get away with a small lie I have told, when I stand in line in a government office holding a document moist with sweat in my hand, when I see children playing soccer in the street, when I have my hair cut, when I look at pictures of pashas and fruit hanging in greengrocers' stalls in Istanbul, when I fail my driving test, when I feel sad after everyone has left the resort at the end of summer, when I am unable to get up and leave at the end of a long visit to someone's home despite the lateness of the hour, when I switch off the chatter of the TV while sitting in a doctor's waiting room, when I run into an old friend from military service, or when there is a sudden silence in the middle of an entertaining conversation. I was never embarrassed when my readers thought that the adventures of my heroes had happened to me as well, because I knew this wasn't true. What's more, I had the support of three centuries of theory of the novel and of fiction, which I could use to shield and protect myself against these claims. And I was well aware that the theory of the novel existed to defend and maintain this independence of imagination from reality. But when an intelligent reader told me she had sensed the real-life experience in the novel's details that "made them mine," I felt embarrassed, like someone who has confessed intimate things about his soul, like someone whose written confessions have been read by another.

I was all the more embarrassed because I was speaking to a reader in a Muslim country, where it is not common practice to talk about your private life in what Jürgen Habermas calls the "public sphere," and where no one writes books like Rousseau's *Confessions*. Like many novelists, not only in controlled societies but in every corner of the world, I actually wanted to share with the reader many things about my sensory experiences, and wanted to express these experiences via fictional characters. All the works of a novelist are like constellations of stars in which he or she offers tens of thousands of small observations about life—in other words, life experiences based on personal sensations. These sensory moments, which encompass everything from opening a door to remembering a long-ago lover, form the irreducible moments of inspiration, the personal points of creativity in novels. In this way, the information the writer has gleaned directly from life experiences—what we call novelistic detail—fuses with the imagination in such a way that the two things become difficult to separate.

Let us remember Jorge Luis Borges's interpretation of Kafka's letter to Max Brod, in which Kafka asked that all his unpublished manuscripts be burned. As Borges put it: When Kafka sent these instructions to Brod, he thought that Brod would not actually burn his manuscripts. Brod, in turn, thought that Kafka was thinking that he was thinking exactly that. And Kafka was thinking that Brod was thinking that he was thinking . . . ad infinitum.

The ambiguity about which parts of the novel are

based on experience and which parts are imagined puts the reader and the writer in a situation similar to this. At every detail, the writer thinks the reader will think that this detail was experienced. And the reader thinks that the writer wrote with the thought that the reader will think that it has been experienced. The writer, in turn, thinks that the reader thinks he wrote that detail thinking that the reader will have thought of this, too. This play of mirrors is valid for the writer's imagination as well. When a writer composes a sentence, he assumes that the reader will (rightly or wrongly) think he has made up this detail. The reader also assumes this, and thinks that the writer assumes that he will likewise think this detail was imaginary. And in the same way, the writer assumes . . . and so on.

Our reading of novels is colored by the uncertainty resulting from this play of mirrors. Just as we cannot agree on what part of the novel is based on experience and what part is imagined, the reader and writer can never agree on the fictionality of the novel. We explain this disagreement by referring to culture, and the difference between the reader's and the writer's understandings of the novel. We complain that in the almost three hundred years that have passed since *Robinson Crusoe,* a common understanding of fiction has still not been established between novelists and readers. But our complaints do not entirely ring true. They lack authenticity; they remind us that they are made in bad faith. Because in a corner of our mind we know that this lack of perfect agreement between the reader and the writer is the driving force of novels.

I'll give one last example to illustrate how important this ambiguity is. Let us imagine that an author writes an autobiography in the first-person singular, and does so with complete honesty, making sure all the details of his life, hundreds of thousands of them, are faithful to his life experience. And let us imagine that a clever publisher brings out the book, calling it a "novel" (there are many clever publishers who might do this). As soon as it is called a novel, we begin to read the book very differently from the way the writer intended. We start looking for a center, wondering about the authenticity of details, asking ourselves which part is real, which part imagined. We do so because we read novels to feel this joy, this pleasure of seeking the center—as well as to speculate about the life-content of the details, and to ask ourselves which are imagined and which are based on experience.

Now, I should mention that this great joy of writing and reading novels is obstructed or bypassed by two kinds of readers:

1. Completely naive readers, who always read a text as an autobiography or as a sort of a disguised chronicle of lived experience, no matter how many times you warn them that they are reading a novel.

2. Completely sentimental-reflective readers, who think that all texts are constructs and fictions anyway, no matter how many times you warn them that they are reading your most candid autobiography.

I must warn you to keep away from such people, because they are immune to the joys of reading novels.

3

Literary Character, Plot, Time

It was by taking novels seriously in my youth that I learned to take life seriously. Literary novels persuade us to take life seriously by showing that we in fact have the power to influence events and that our personal decisions shape our lives. In closed or semi-closed societies, where individual choice is restricted, the art of the novel remains underdeveloped. But whenever the art of the novel does develop in these societies, it invites people to examine their lives, and it achieves this by presenting meticulously constructed literary narratives about individuals' personal traits, sensations, and decisions. When we leave aside traditional narratives and begin to read novels, we come to feel that our own world and our choices can be as important as historical events, international wars, and the decisions of kings, pashas, armies, governments, and gods—and that, even more remarkably, our sensations and thoughts have the potential to be far more interesting than any of these. As I devoured novels in my youth, I felt a breathtaking sense of freedom and self-confidence.

This is the point at which literary characters enter

the picture, because reading a novel means looking at the world through the eyes, mind, and soul of the novel's characters. The stories, romances, epics, *masnavis* (tales told in rhyming couplets, in Turkish, Persian, Arabic, or Urdu), and long poetic narratives of premodern times typically describe the world from the reader's point of view. In these old narratives, the hero is generally set within a landscape, and we the readers are outside it. The novel, in contrast, invites us into the landscape. We see the universe from the hero's point of view—through his sensations and, when possible, through his words. (In the case of the historical novel, this sort of representation is limited because the character's language must fit naturally within the context of the period. The historical novel works best when its artifices and framing devices are apparent.) Seen through the eyes of its characters, the world of the novel seems closer and more comprehensible to us. It is this proximity that lends the art of the novel its irresistible power. Yet the primary focus is not the personality and morality of the leading characters, but the nature of their world. The life of the protagonists, their place in the world, the way they feel, see, and engage with their world—*this* is the subject of the literary novel.

In our daily lives, we are curious about the character of our city's newly elected mayor. Likewise, we want to know about the new teacher at the school we attend. Is he tough on his students? Are his exams fair? Is he kindhearted? The character of our new officemate at work has a big impact on our life, too. We are curious about these "characters" we encounter—that is, we are curious about their values, tastes, and habits, as opposed to the way they look. And we all know what a powerful influence the character of our parents has on us (though of course their material circumstances and level of education matter as well). Of course, the choice of a life partner is a reasonable and compelling topic, both in life and in narrative, ranging from Jane Austen to the present, from *Anna Karenina* to today's popular films. I'm mentioning all these examples to remind you that, because life is challenging and difficult, we have a strong and legitimate curiosity about the habits and values of the people around us. And the source of our curiosity is by no means literary. (This curiosity also motivates our fondness for gossip and for the latest news from the grapevine.) The novel's strong emphasis on character likewise springs from this very human curiosity. Indeed, over the past one hundred fifty years, this curiosity has taken up much more space in the novel than it has in life. It has sometimes become too self-indulgent, almost vulgar.

For Homer, character was a defining attribute, an essential quality that never altered. Despite moments of fear and indecision, Odysseus is always great-hearted. In contrast, for the seventeenth-century Ottoman travel writer Evliya Çelebi, as for many other writers of the period, the character of the people was a natural feature of the cities he visited, like the climate, the water, and the topography. He would mention in the same breath, for instance, that the climate of Trebizond was rainy, its men were tough, and its women were tough as well. To-day we simply smile at the idea that all the inhabitants of a city share the same character traits. But let's re-member that newspaper horoscopes, which are read and believed by millions of people, are based on the naive view that individuals born around the same time will share the same personality.

Like many people, I believe that Shakespeare is re-sponsible for our conception of the modern fictional character, developed initially in a broad range of lit-erary writings and later in the nineteenth-century novel. Shakespeare, and Shakespeare criticism in par-ticular, helped the fictional character to evolve from its centuries-old definition—the embodiment of a single basic attribute, a one-dimensional role, historical or symbolic in nature (despite Molière's brilliant wit, the protagonist of his play *The Miser* is always and only a miser)—and transformed it into a complex entity

shaped by conflicting impulses and conditions. Dostoyevsky's understanding of human nature is a perfect
illustration of our modern notions of the human being—that intricate bundle of qualities which cannot be
reduced to anything else. Yet "character" in Dostoyevsky has become much stronger and more determining
than any other aspect of life; it dominates the novel and
leaves an indelible stamp on it. We read Dostoyevsky to
understand the protagonists, not life itself. Reading and
discussing *The Brothers Karamazov,* that truly great
novel, becomes, through the three brothers and their
half-brother, a discussion of four types of people, four
types of character. Just like Schiller ruminating on naive
and sentimental character types, we are completely absorbed when reading Dostoyevsky. But at the same time
we think: *Life isn't quite like this.*

Influenced by scientific discoveries about the laws of
nature, and later by the philosophy of positivism,
nineteenth-century novelists began to investigate the
secret souls of modern individuals, creating a splendid
array of heroes and consistent characters—"types" that
represented various facets of society. In his highly influential *Aspects of the Novel,* which deals with the success
and qualities of the nineteenth-century novel, E. M.
Forster devoted the largest part of his attention to the
topic of character and the varieties of novelistic heroes,

classifying them and describing how they developed. Reading this book in my twenties, when I felt a very strong desire to become a novelist, I sensed that human character was not nearly as important in real life as Forster said it was in literature. But I would then go on to think: *If it's important in novels, it must be important in life too—after all, I don't know much about life.* Yet I also concluded that a successful novelist had to create an unforgettable hero like Tom Jones, Ivan Karamazov, Madame Bovary, Père Goriot, Anna Karenina, or Oliver Twist. In my youth I aspired to this goal—but later on, I never titled any of my novels after its hero.

The excessive and disproportionate interest shown in the traits and quirks of novelistic heroes spread, just like the novel itself, from Europe to the rest of the world. Seeing, as they did, the people and stories of their own countries through the devices of the new foreign toy called the "novel," novelists outside Europe in the late nineteenth century and throughout the twentieth century felt obliged to create an Ivan Karamazov or a Don Quixote in their own cultures. Turkish critics of the 1950s and 1960s would proudly sing the praises of the provincial writers they admired by declaring, "This novel shows that even in a poor Turkish village we may find a Hamlet or an Ivan Karamazov." The fact that the most brilliant novella by the Russian writer Nikolai

Leskov, whom Walter Benjamin greatly admired, was entitled *Lady Macbeth of Mstensk* should remind us how widespread the problem was. (The main inspiration for this novel was actually *Madame Bovary,* rather than *Macbeth.*) Viewing the literary figures created in the cultural centers of the West as die-cast artifacts, and transporting them—just like Duchampian ready-made art objects—to non-Western countries, where the art of the novel was just blossoming, filled these authors with pride and satisfaction. They felt that the character of their nation's people was as deep and complex as that of Westerners.

So, for a great many years, it was as if the entire community of world literature and critical thought forgot that what we call "character" was, especially in novels, a figment of the human imagination, an artificial construct. Recall, once again, that Schiller used the word "naive" to describe those people who fail to see the artifice in things, and let's ask ourselves naively how the world of literature managed to remain so silent and so naive with regard to the character of literary protagonists. Was this a result of the prevailing interest in psychology—a field that had acquired a scientific aura and that, in the first half of the twentieth century, quickly spread among writers like a contagious disease? Or was it due to a wave of naive and vulgar humanistic enthusiasm which supported the notion that people were essentially the same everywhere? Or was it perhaps attributable to the hegemony of Western literature in relation to literatures on the periphery, where the readership was small?

The most generally accepted reason, which also happens to be the one that Forster advocated, is that literary characters take over the plot, the setting, and the themes when the novel is being written. This view, which has aspects bordering on the mystical, is an article of faith among many writers, who treat it as if it were God's own truth. The primary task of the novelist, they believe, is to invent a hero! Once the author successfully achieves this, the hero, like a prompter on a stage, will whisper to the novelist the entire course of the novel. Forster goes so far as to suggest that we novelists must learn from this literary character what we are to narrate in the book. This view does not prove the importance of human character in our lives. It merely goes to show that many novelists begin to write their novels without being sure of their story, and that this is the only way they are able to write. Moreover, it points to the most challenging aspect of writing, and also of reading: the fact that a novel is the product of both an art and a craft. The longer the novel, the more difficult it is for the author to plan the details, keep them all in his mind, and successfully create a perception of the story's center.

Such views, which place heroes and their traits at the heart of the novel, have been accepted so naively and uncritically that they are taught as rules and methods in creative-writing courses. When I was reading and doing research in some of America's great libraries, as preparation for writing these lectures, I found very little by way of acknowledgment that the aspect of the human being we call "character" is a historical construct, and that, just like our own psychological and emotional makeup, the character of literary figures is an artifice we choose to believe in. Just like gossip about the character of people we know in real life, eloquent speeches celebrating the unforgettable nature of certain literary heroes are often nothing more than empty rhetoric.

Since I believe that the essential aim of the art of the novel is to present an accurate depiction of life, let me be forthright. People do not actually have as much character as we find portrayed in novels, especially in nineteenth- and twentieth-century novels. I am fifty-seven years old as I write these words. I have never been able to identify in myself the kind of character I encounter in novels—or rather, European novels. Furthermore, human character is not nearly as important in the shaping of our lives as it is made out to be in the

novels and literary criticism of the West. To say that
character-creation should be the primary goal of the
novelist runs counter to what we know about everyday
human life.

Yet having a character, like having a personal style in
post-Renaissance painting, does confer distinctiveness
on a person: it sets that individual apart from others.
But more decisive than the character of a novel's protagonists is how they fit into the surrounding landscape, events, and milieu.

The strongest initial urges I feel when writing a novel
are to make sure I can "see" in words some of the topics and themes, to explore an aspect of life that has
never before been depicted, and to be the first to put
into words the feelings, thoughts, and circumstances
that people who live in the same universe as me are experiencing. In the beginning, there are patterns formed
by people, objects, stories, images, situations, beliefs,
history, and the juxtaposition of all these things—in
other words, a texture—as well as situations I want to
dramatize, emphasize, and delve into more deeply.
Whether my literary figures have a strong character or
a mild character (like mine), I need them to explore
new realms and new ideas. The character of my novel's
main protagonist is determined the same way a person's
character is formed in life: by the situations and events

he lives through. The story or plot is a line that effectively connects the various circumstances I want to narrate. The protagonist is someone who is shaped by these situations and who helps to elucidate them in a telling way.

Whether my protagonists resemble me or not, I make every effort to identify with them. I imagine them into being, little by little, so as to see the world of the novel through their eyes. The defining question of the art of the novel is not the personality or character of the protagonists, but rather how the universe within the tale appears to them. If we are to understand someone and make moral observations about the person, we must comprehend how the world appears from that person's vantage point. And for this, we need both information and imagination. The art of the novel becomes political not when the author expresses political views, but when we make an effort to understand someone who is different from us in terms of culture, class, and gender. This means feeling compassion before passing ethical, cultural, or political judgment.

The author's identification with the heroes of his books has a childlike quality to it, especially during the sentence-by-sentence process of writing. Childlike, but not naive. My mood, as I identify with each of my heroes, resembles what I used to feel when I played alone as a child. Like all children, I liked to play make-believe, to put myself in someone else's place and imagine dream worlds in which I was a soldier, a famous soccer player, or a great hero. (Jean-Paul Sartre, in his autobiography *Les Mots,* or *The Words,* poetically captures the resemblance between a child's act of make-believe and the mindset of a novelist.) The structural games of the novel I am composing add a further childlike joy to the pleasure I derive from writing. In the thirty-five years that I've made my living by writing novels, I've often felt fortunate to have a job that involves playing games like those I used to play as a child. Despite all its challenges and the great labor it demands, being a novelist has always seemed a joyful business to me.

The process of identification is childlike, but it is not entirely naive, because it cannot occupy my mind completely. While one corner of my mind is busy creating fictional people, speaking and acting like my heroes, and generally trying to inhabit another person's skin, a different corner of my mind is carefully assessing the novel as a whole—surveying the overall composition, gauging how the reader will read, interpreting the narrative and the actors, and trying to predict the effect of my sentences. All of these subtle calculations, involving the contrived aspect of the novel and the sentimental-reflective side of the novelist, reveal a self-consciousness that is in direct contrast to the naïveté of childhood. The more the novelist succeeds in simultaneously being both naive and sentimental, the better he writes.

A good example of the clash—or concordance—between the novelist's naive side (childlike, playful, capable of identifying with others) and his sentimental-reflective side (aware of his own voice and absorbed in technical issues) is the fact that each novelist knows there are limits to his ability to identify with others. The art of the novel is the knack of being able to speak about ourselves as if we were another person, and about others as if we were in their shoes. And just as there is a limit to the extent we can speak about ourselves as if we were another person, there is also a limit to how much we can identify with another person. The desire to create the many possible types of heroes by overcoming all differences of culture, history, class, and gender—to transcend ourselves in order to see and discover the whole—is a basic liberatory urge that makes writing and reading novels attractive, as well as an aspiration that makes us realize the limits of one human being's ability to understand another.

There is something so special about the facet of writing and reading novels that relates to freedom, to imitating other lives and imagining oneself as another person, that I would like to dwell a little on this ethical point. One of the most enjoyable aspects of writing novels is the discovery that as the novelist deliberately puts himself in the place of his characters, and as he carries out research and uses his imagination, he slowly changes himself. Not only does he see the world through the eyes of his hero, but he gradually comes to resemble his hero! Another reason I love the art of writing novels is that it forces me to go beyond my own point of view and become someone else. As a novelist, I have identified with others and stepped outside the bounds of my self, acquiring a character I did not formerly possess. Over the past thirty-five years, by writing novels and putting myself in the place of others, I have created a finer and more complex version of myself.

To go beyond the limits of our selves, to perceive everyone and everything as a great whole, to identify with as many people as possible, to see as much as possible: in this way, the novelist comes to resemble those ancient Chinese painters who climbed mountain peaks in order to capture the poetry of vast landscapes. Scholars of Chinese landscape painting, such as James Cahill, like to remind naive enthusiasts that the viewpoint which encompasses everything from high above in a single glance and makes these paintings possible is actually imaginary, and that no painter really creates his artworks on a mountaintop. Likewise, the composition of a novel entails the search for an imaginary point from which one can see the whole. This imaginary vantage point is also the spot from which one can most clearly perceive the novel's center.

When a fictional person wanders through a great landscape, inhabits it, engages with it, and becomes part of it—these are the gestures that make him or her unforgettable. Anna Karenina is memorable not because of the fluctuations of her soul or the cluster of attributes we call "character," but because of the broad, rich landscape that she is so deeply immersed in and that, in turn, reveals itself through her in all its sumptuous detail. Reading the novel, we both see the landscape through the heroine's eyes and know that the heroine is part of the wealth of that landscape. Later on, she will be transformed into an unforgettable sign, a kind of emblem that reminds us of the landscape she is part of. The fact that long, rich novels like *Don Quixote, David Copperfield,* and *Anna Karenina* bear the names of their main characters emphasizes the quasi-emblematic task of the protagonist: to evoke the entire landscape in the mind of the reader. What remains in our mind is often the novel's general layout or comprehensive world, which I refer to as its "landscape." But the protagonist is the element we feel we remember. So in our imagination his or her name becomes the name of the landscape the novel presents to us.

This time-honored way of rendering protagonists—as a part of the landscape they inhabit—was described by Coleridge in his lectures on Shakespeare: "The characters of the 'dramatis personae,' like those in real life, are to be inferred by the reader; they are not told to him." Coleridge's observation had far-reaching effects. Almost eight generations of novel writers and readers—I mean over a span of nearly two hundred years—concluded that the primary challenge of the novelistic art was the construction of the protagonist's character, and the successful discovery of that character by the reader.

Let us remember that Coleridge wrote these words approximately two centuries after Shakespeare, as the English novel was on the rise and Dickens was about to write his first novels. But the challenge and deep joy provided by the novel come not when we infer the character of the protagonist from his behavior, but when we *identify* with him, within at least a part of our soul—and in this way, even if only temporarily, break free of our selves, become another person, and for once see the world through someone else's eyes. If the real task of the novel is to describe what it feels like to live in the world, then of course this relates closely to human character and psychology. But the novel's subject is more interesting than mere psychology. What matters is not the individual's character, but the way in which he or she reacts to the manifold forms of the world— each color, each event, each fruit and blossom, everything our senses bring to us. And our feeling of identification with the protagonist, which is the main pleasure and reward afforded by the art of the novel, is based on these very sensations.

It is not because Anna Karenina has any particular type of character that Tolstoy depicts her as behaving in a certain way on the Moscow–St. Petersburg train. He simply relates the feelings of an unhappily married woman riding home on a train with a novel in her hand, after she's danced with a handsome young military officer at a ball in Moscow. What makes Anna unforgettable is the accuracy of the myriad small details. We come to see, feel, and engage with everything just as much as she does—the snowy night outside, the interior of the compartment, the novel she is reading (or trying unsuccessfully to read). We see, feel, and show interest just like her. Perhaps one reason for this is the way Tolstoy shapes her character: in contrast to the way Cervantes portrays Don Quixote, Tolstoy presents Anna as soft, ambiguous, allowing enough space for us to identify with her. We are not left standing outside when we read *Anna Karenina,* as we are when we read *Don Quixote.* The most distinctive aspect of the art of the novel is that it shows the world the way the protagonists perceive it, with all of their senses. And since the broad landscape we view from afar is described through their eyes and through their senses, we put ourselves in their place, are deeply moved, and migrate from one figure's perspective to another to comprehend the general landscape as a feeling experienced from within. The landscape the figures walk through does not cast a shadow on them; on the contrary, the novel's protagonists have been imagined and constructed for the precise purpose of revealing the details of this landscape and illuminating it. To do this, they must become deeply involved with the world they perceive.

The techniques of portraying their involvement will be this lecture's second and third subjects: plot and time in the novel. To say that the character or the soul of the protagonists is *not* the real subject of the novel, we have to turn away from the naive side of our mind and bring out, in a sentimental-reflective way, the artifice of character portrayal. This artifice is the basis for our construction and understanding of literary figures. The novelist develops his heroes in accordance with the topics he wants to research, explore, and relate,

and with the life experiences he wishes to make the focus of his imagination and creativity.

Novelists do not first invent a protagonist with a very
special soul, and then get pulled along, according to the
wishes of this figure, into specific subjects or experiences. The desire to explore particular topics comes
first. Only then do novelists conceive the figures who
would be most suitable for elucidating these topics.
This is how I have always done it. And I feel that all
writers, knowingly or unknowingly, do the same.

The statement, "That is how I have always done it!"
could have been the subtitle of these lectures. My intent here is to explain my understanding of the genre
known as the "novel." How did my imagination engage with this particular genre, which was developed,
shaped, and placed before me like a wonderful toy—
a three-dimensional universe composed of words by
thousands of previous writers? What is the emotional
and intellectual heart of my work as a novelist? My
point of view is similar to that of a cautious but opti-
mistic humanist, who thinks he can portray all humanity insofar as he can understand himself and manage to
express his self-understanding. I naively believe I can
show how the minds of other novelists function when
those writers construct a novel, so long as I sincerely

convey my own experience of reading and writing novels. In other words, there is a naive side of me that believes I can express to you, my readers, the sentimental-reflective side of my being which is preoccupied with the technical aspects of the novel.

With regard to this naive side of my nature, I feel an affinity for the narrative theories of the early twentieth-century Russian Formalists, such as Viktor Shklovsky. What we call "plot," the sequence of events in the story, is nothing but a line that connects the points we want to relate and pass through. This line does not represent the material or the content of the novel—that is, the novel itself. Rather, it indicates the distribution throughout the text of the many thousands of small points that compose the novel. Narrative units, subjects, patterns, subplots, mini-stories, poetic moments, personal experiences, bits of information—whatever you choose to call such points, *these* are the large and small spheres of energy that urge and encourage me to write a novel. In an essay on *Lolita,* Vladimir Nabokov called these most significant, most unforgettable points the "nerve endings" that make up a book. I feel that these units are, just like Aristotle's atoms, indivisible and irreducible entities.

In my novel *The Museum of Innocence,* drawing on Aristotle's *Physics,* I tried to establish a relationship be-

tween these indivisible points and the moments that
make up Time. According to Aristotle, just as there are
indivisible and irreducible atoms, there are also indivisible moments; and the line that connects these countless moments is called Time. In the same way, the plot
of a novel is the line that connects the large and small
indivisible narrative units. Naturally, the protagonists
must possess the soul, character, and psychological
makeup to justify the trajectory and drama required by
this line, by the plot.

The main quality that separates the novel from other
long narratives and that makes it such a widely loved
genre is the way it is read: the act of seeing each of
these small points, these nerve endings along the line,
through the eyes of one of the figures in the story, and
the process of associating these points with the feelings and perceptions of the protagonists. Whether the
events are told in the first person or the third person,
whether the novelist or the narrator is aware or unaware of this relationship, the reader absorbs every detail in the general landscape by associating it with the
emotions and moods of a protagonist close to the
events. This, then, is the golden rule of the art of the
novel, stemming from the novel's own inner structure:
the reader should be left with the impression that even
a description of a setting entirely devoid of people or

an object completely peripheral to the story is a necessary extension of the emotional, sensual, and psychological world of the protagonists. Though ordinary logic suggests that what Anna Karenina sees in the landscape outside the train window might be coincidental, and that the train may pass through any type of scenery, while we're reading the novel the snowflakes outside the train window reflect the mood of the young woman to us. After dancing with the handsome officer at a ball in Moscow, Anna has settled into her compartment and is on her way back to the security of her home and family—but her mind is focused on the adventure beyond, on the frightening power and beauty of nature. In a good novel, a great novel, descriptions of the landscape, various objects, embedded tales, slight digressions—everything makes us feel the moods, habits, and character of the protagonists. Let us imagine a novel as a sea made up of these irreducible nerve endings, these moments—the units that inspire the writer —and let us never forget that every point contains a bit of the protagonists' soul.

Time, as Aristotle describes it in his *Physics,* is a straight line connecting discrete moments. This is objective time, known and agreed upon by all, and kept track of by means of calendars and clocks. In contrast to other long fictional genres and to histories, novels portray the world from the point of view of the people who live inside it, through the details of their souls and their sensibilities—and thus, in novels, time is not the linear and objective time indicated by Aristotle, but the subjective time of the protagonists. Yet in order to determine the relationships among the protagonists, we readers still try to discern—especially when reading densely populated novels—the objective time shared by everyone in the novel. Sincere and naive writers, who are untroubled by the artifice of narrative techniques, provide their readers with explanatory sentences such as, "Around the time that Anna boarded the Moscow train, Levin on his estate . . . ," to help us construct objective time in our imagination. But there's not always a need for such prompts from the narrator. The reader can imagine the shared objective time of the novel with the aid of events such as snowfalls, storms, earthquakes, fires, wars, church bells, calls to prayer, changes of season, epidemics, newspaper accounts, and major public events—phenomena that all the protagonists know about, even those who are not in direct contact with one another. This process of imagining is political, in that it is similar to the way we might imagine a group that *represents* the people in the novel, or a city crowd, or a community, or a nation; and it is at this juncture that the novel is furthest from poetry and the inner demons of its protagonists, and closest to history. To feel, when reading a novel, the existence of a shared objective time evokes in us an emotion that resembles the pleasure we feel when we look at a large landscape painting and see everything simultaneously: we think we have found the secret center of the novel in the folds of history and the characteristics of a community. But I believe this is misleading. In Tolstoy's *War and Peace* and James Joyce's *Ulysses,* two novels in which we quite often feel the presence of shared objective time, the deep, secret center is related not to history, but to life itself and its structure.

What we call "objective time" functions as a frame that unites the elements of the novel and makes them seem as if they're in a landscape painting. But this frame is hard to distinguish, and readers thus need the help of the narrator—because during both the writing and the reading of the novel, the narrative (unlike a landscape painting) requires that we see not the general landscape, but what each individual figure sees and perceives, and that we appreciate all these limited points of view. In a well-executed classical Chinese landscape painting, we simultaneously see the individual trees, the forest they are a part of, and the general landscape. But in the case of the novel, it is difficult for both the writer and the readers to distance themselves from the protagonists in order to distinguish objective time and get an overall view of the novel.

Anna Karenina is one of the most perfect novels ever conceived. And those who know how Tolstoy composed it—through incessant revising, correcting, and polishing—know that it is also a book written with great care. Yet Nabokov has shown—while reveling in the pleasure of appearing even more intelligent than Tolstoy—that although there are few mistakes in the individual stories of the protagonists, Tolstoy failed to effectively structure the shared objective time in *Anna Karenina,* and that the calendars of the protagonists do not match up—in other words, that the novel contains many chronological errors which a careful editor would have noticed. Those who read the novel for sheer pleasure won't notice these inconsistencies; they will assume that Tolstoy's calendars are accurate. This carelessness on the part of the writer and his readers stems from the habit of writing and reading novels with a focus on the protagonists' time rather than on the general time of the landscape—a habit that is understandable, because reading a novel involves entering the landscape and missing the general picture.

After Conrad, Proust, Joyce, Faulkner, and Virginia Woolf, leaps in plot or time became an accepted part of the technique of revealing to the reader the character, habits, and moods of a novel's protagonists. These modernist writers—who arranged events in the general landscape not according to the linear sequence of clocks and calendars, but according to the protagonists' memories, their role in the drama, and, most important, their beliefs and instincts—made readers all over the world (the novel had by then become a world art!) feel that an alternate way of understanding their own life and comprehending its uniqueness was to pay attention to their *subjective* experience of time. As we have come to discover—with the help of the modern novel—the importance of our own personal Time and moments, we have also learned to see the hero's character, his psychological and emotional traits, as part of the general landscape of the novel. Understanding, through the vehicle of the novel, the small details of life that we had previously overlooked means placing them, imbued with meaning, into the general landscape and the context of history. It is only by entering the general landscape through the minute details of our life and our emotions that we acquire the strength and freedom to understand at all.

The snowflakes seen from the train window can tell us about Anna Karenina's mood because she has been made vulnerable by a young military officer at a ball in Moscow, and has been moved to such an extent that she considers entering into an emotional relationship with him. Inventing and constructing the character of a protagonist entails combining the plot with the irreducible details from real life that are familiar to all of us. For me, writing a novel means being able to detect within the landscape (the world) my characters' moods, emotions, and thoughts. So I always feel that I should connect the thousands of small dots that compose a novel not by drawing a straight line, but by drawing zigzags between them. In a novel, objects, furniture, rooms, streets, landscapes, trees, the forest, the weather, the view outside the window—everything appears to us as a function of the protagonists' thoughts and feelings, formed from the general landscape of the novel.

4

Words, Pictures, Objects

I have said that the art of writing novels is the ability to perceive the thoughts and sensations of protagonists within a landscape—that is, amid the surrounding objects and images. This ability is less important in the art of some novelists, the best example being Dostoyevsky. Reading Dostoyevsky's novels, we sometimes feel that we have encountered something surprisingly profound —that we have attained a truly deep knowledge of life, of people, and above all of our own selves. This knowledge seems so familiar and at the same time so extraordinary, that it occasionally fills us with fear.

The knowledge or wisdom that Dostoyevsky provides us speaks not to our visual imagination, but to our verbal imagination. With regard to the power of the novel and an understanding of the human psyche, Tolstoy is sometimes equally profound; and because these two men wrote during the same period and within the same culture, they are invariably compared with each other. Yet the greater part of Tolstoy's insights are different in kind from Dostoyevsky's. Tolstoy addresses not just our verbal imagination, but—even more—our visual imagination.

No doubt every literary text addresses both our visual and textual intelligence. In live theater, where everything takes place in front of our eyes and for the pleasure of our eyes, wordplay, analytical thought, the joys of poetic language, and the flow of everyday speech are also, of course, part of the pleasure. In the case of an exceedingly dramatic writer like Dostoyevsky—say, in the suicide scene in *The Devils*—there may be no explicit image on the page (the reader has to imagine, along with the hero, someone committing suicide in the room next door), yet the scene leaves a strong visual impression on us. Still, despite all the tension that sets the reader's head spinning—or perhaps because of it— only a few objects, images, and scenes from Dostoyevsky's work actually stick in our mind. Whereas Tolstoy's world is teeming with suggestive, subtly placed objects, Dostoyevsky's rooms almost seem to be empty.

Allow me to generalize here, so that I can more easily explain my point. Some writers are better at addressing our verbal imagination, while others speak more powerfully to our visual imagination. I will call the first kind "verbal writers" and the second kind "visual writers." Homer, for me, is a visual writer: as I read him, countless images pass before my eyes. I enjoy these images more than the story itself. But Ferdowsi, the author of the great Persian epic *Shahnameh,* which I read over and over while writing the novel *My Name Is Red,* is a verbal writer who mainly relies on the plot and its twists and turns. Of course, no writer can be placed solely on one side or the other of such a divide. But while reading some writers, we become more engaged with words, with the course of the dialogue, with the paradoxes or thoughts the narrator is exploring, whereas other writers impress us by filling our minds with indelible images, visions, landscapes, and objects.

Coleridge is the best example of a writer who can be either visual or verbal, depending on the genre he is employing. In his poetry—for instance, in *The Rime of the Ancient Mariner*—he is a poet who, rather than telling a story, paints a series of splendid pictures for the reader. But in his prose, personal journals, and autobiography, Coleridge becomes an analytical writer who expects us to think entirely in concepts and words. Moreover, he is able to describe, with great insight, how he created his poems: he wrote them with his visual imagination, while analyzing them with his verbal imagination—see, for example, the fourth chapter of his *Biographia Literaria.* In the same way, Edgar Allan Poe, who learned a great deal from Coleridge, explains in his essay "The Philosophy of Composition" that he wrote his poem "The Raven" by addressing the reader's textual imagination.

In order to understand the dichotomy between what I call "visual literature" and "verbal literature," let's close our eyes for a moment, focus on a subject, and allow a thought to form in our mind. Then let's open our eyes and ask ourselves: As we were thinking, what passed through our mind—words or images? The answer can be either, or both. We feel that sometimes we think in words, and sometimes in images. Often we switch from one to the other. My aim here is to show, by using this distinction between the visual and the verbal, that any particular literary text tends to exercise one of these centers in our brain more than the other.

Here is one of my strongest opinions: novels are essentially *visual* literary fictions. A novel exerts its influence on us mostly by addressing our visual intelligence —our ability to see things in our mind's eye and to turn words into mental pictures. We all know that, in contrast to other literary genres, novels rely on our memory of ordinary life experiences and of sensory impressions we sometimes do not even notice. In addition to depicting the world, novels also describe—with a richness that no other literary form can rival—the feelings evoked by our senses of smell, sound, taste, and touch. The general landscape of the novel comes to life—beyond what the protagonists see—with that world's sounds, smells, tastes, and moments of contact. Yet among the experiences of living that each of us feels from moment to moment in our own unique way, seeing is no doubt the most significant. Writing a novel means painting with words, and reading a novel means visualizing images through someone else's words.

By "painting with words," I mean evoking a very clear and distinct image in the mind of the reader through the use of words. When I am writing a novel, sentence by sentence, word by word (dialogue scenes aside), the first step is always the formation of a picture, an image, in my mind. I am aware that my immediate task is to clarify and bring into focus this mental image. From reading biographies and writers' memoirs, and from conversing with other novelists, I've come to realize that—compared to other writers—I put more effort into planning before I put pen to paper. I take somewhat greater care to divide a book into sections and structure it. When I write a chapter, a scene, or a small tableau (you see that the vocabulary of painting comes naturally to me!), I first see it in detail in my mind's eye. For me, writing is the process of visualizing that particular scene, that picture. I gaze out the window just as much as I look down at the page I am writing on with a fountain pen. As I prepare to transform my thoughts into words, I strive to visualize each scene like a film sequence, and each sentence like a painting.

But the analogies of film and painting are valid only up to a point. When I am about to describe a scene, I try to envision and highlight the aspect of it that can be expressed in the most succinct and powerful way. As my visual imagination constructs the chapter I am writing, scene by scene and sentence by sentence, it focuses on those details that can be expressed most effectively in words. Sometimes I recall a detail from real life, and visualize it—but then, realizing I cannot express it in words, I abandon it. This feeling of insufficiency often results from my belief that my experience is unique to me alone. I'm searching for the right word —"le mot juste" that Flaubert said he sought when he wrote (in fact, before he sat down to write)—that can best convey the image in my mind. The novelist not only seeks the word that best expresses what he visualizes, but also gradually learns how to visualize the things he is good at verbalizing. (Such a well-chosen image should be called *l'image juste*—"the right image.") The novelist feels that the image he sees in his mind's eye can acquire meaning only when he transforms it into words, and that the visual and verbal centers in his brain are moving closer to each other, the more he learns to visualize the things he can recast into

words. These centers are perhaps nested one inside the
other, and not located on opposite sides of the brain.

It has become conventional to cite the famous line
"Ut pictura poesis" ("As is painting, so is poetry"),
from Horace's *Ars Poetica,* whenever one evokes the
kinship between words and images or between literature and painting. I also like the lesser-known words
that follow this statement (Horace comes out with
them unexpectedly after declaring that even Homer
could compose inferior verse), because they remind me
that looking at a landscape painting is much like reading a novel. I quote from the prose translation by D. A.
Russell: "Poetry is like painting. Some attracts you
more if you stand near, some if you're further off. One
picture likes a dark place; one will need to be seen in
the light, because it's not afraid of the critic's sharp
judgment. One gives pleasure once; one will please if
you look it over ten times."

Horace uses the analogy and vocabulary of painting
elsewhere in *Ars Poetica,* as well, but there his ideas and
examples do not go beyond mentioning the way in
which the pleasures of poetry resemble those of painting. The real difference between the arts of literature
and painting was formulated, via analytical logic, by the
German dramatist and critic Gotthold Ephraim Lessing
in his book *Laocoön* (1766). Subtitled *An Essay on the*

Limits of Painting and Poetry, this work presents the distinction that today everyone agrees on: poetry (literature) is an art that unfolds in time, whereas painting, sculpture, and the other visual arts unfold in space. Time and Space are essential Kantian categories.

Looking at a landscape painting, we instantly grasp the general meaning: everything is displayed right there before us. But in order to grasp the general meaning of a poem or a prose narrative, we need to understand how the protagonists and circumstances change over time—in other words, we must understand the story, the drama, and the events. The events are situated in the context of dramatic time. And we need time to read verbal compositions, in order to follow their structure.

Actually, if we are to appreciate a detailed landscape painting, we must also—just as Horace said—look at it ten times, view it from various distances, pay attention to its details, and spend time gazing at it. Moreover, paintings that illustrate a story can incorporate within a single frame more than one Time—that is, the sort of Aristotelian moments that I referred to in my previous lecture. One corner of a large-scale painting may depict the incident that triggered a great war, while another corner may show the wounded and the dead that the war left in its wake. This we call "narrative painting," a technique used in the early sixteenth century by European masters such as Carpaccio, as well as by Persian masters of the same period, such as Bihzad.

But these examples do not detract from the validity of the famous distinction made by Lessing. His use of two main philosophical categories, Time and Space, established a clear contrast between poetry and painting (often called the "sister arts" because of their interrelated power to move the human soul). Let me use this distinction to articulate my own view of the novel. Novels, just like paintings, present frozen moments. Yet novels contain more than just one of these small, indivisible moments (much like Aristotelian moments): they offer thousands, tens of thousands of them. When we read a novel, we visualize these word-formed moments, these points of Time. That is, we transform them into Space in our imagination.

When we look at a painting—whether a landscape painting, a book illustration, a manuscript illumination, a portrait miniature, or a still life—we immediately get a general impression. But the situation is precisely the opposite when we read a novel. As we turn the pages, our attention constantly focuses on small details, small pictures, small irreducible moments, and we wait impatiently until we can make out the general landscape, all the while trying to remember the myriad details. Whereas a painting shows us a frozen moment, novels present us with thousands of frozen moments lined up one after the other. Reading a novel can often be quite suspenseful, as our curiosity eagerly tries to determine where each moment fits within the general landscape, and how it may point toward the novel's center. Why is the writer *at this particular moment* showing us the snowflakes seen from the window? Why is he providing such detailed descriptions of the other people in the train compartment? To be wondering where exactly we are in the entire forest of moments, or how we might find our way out of it—while simultaneously examining every tree, every detail, every narrative unit—might make us feel suffocated, as if we're completely lost in the woods. But our attention is sustained by the fact that the trees in the forest, the many thousands of indivisible moments that constitute the story, are made up of ordinary human details which quite often are visual details. What keeps us attentive is the way they appear to the protagonists—in other words, the way they reveal the protagonists' thoughts, emotions, and character.

Looking at a large painting, we feel the thrill of being in the presence of everything all at once, and we want to enter the painting. When we are in the middle of a big novel, we feel the dizzy pleasure of being in a world which we cannot see in its entirety. To see everything, we must continually transform the discrete moments of the novel into pictures in our mind. It is this process of transformation that makes the reading of a novel a more collaborative, more personal task than gazing at a painting.

In conjunction with my friend Andreas Huyssen, I have been teaching a seminar at Columbia University. The purpose of the course is to explore the relationship between literary texts and painting, and to discuss, with examples, how words mobilize our visual imagination. The discussions inevitably touch on what the ancient Greeks called *ekphrasis*. In its first and narrower meaning, ekphrasis is the description of visual artworks (such as paintings and sculptures) through the medium of poetry, for the benefit of those who cannot see them. The paintings and sculptures in the poems can be real or imaginary, just like details in novels. And that's really all you can say about this meaning of the word. The best-known example of ekphrasis in classical literature is the description of the shield of Achilles in Book 18 of the *Iliad*. Homer gives such an extraordinary account of the images forged into the shield by the god Hephaestos—the stars, the sun, the cities, and the people it depicts—that the description becomes a portrait of an entire word-universe, a literary text much more important than the shield itself. Inspired by Homer's description, W. H. Auden wrote a poem entitled "The Shield of Achilles," recasting the ekphrasis from the perspective of twentieth-century wars.

I have included many such descriptions in my books, though not (as Auden did) to pass judgment on an era—in other words, to look at it from a distance—but, on the contrary, to enter into a picture through writing and to become part of the period in which it was created. Especially in *My Name Is Red,* where not only the protagonists but also the colors and objects have voices and speak aloud, I felt that I was entering a different world—a world I wanted to describe and reconstruct via painting. For people living in the present, the past is made of old buildings, old texts, old paintings. Starting not only from texts but also from paintings, and believing that the past could be imagined with sufficient vividness for a novel, I described in detail the paintings in the books and archives of the Topkapı Palace in Istanbul at the end of the sixteenth century—the majority of which, as it happens, were produced in what is now Iran and Afghanistan—and I set out to create a universe by identifying with the heroes, the objects, and even the devils portrayed in those miniatures.

This endeavor persuaded me that there should be a broader interpretation of ekphrasis. Whether we use the classical Greek word "ekphrasis" or the phrase "verbal description," the problem is how to describe, in words, the splendors of the real or imaginary visual world to those who have never seen them. Let us remember that our point of departure is art before the age of photography, and the difficulties posed by an era in which photocopies, prints, and other forms of reproduction were unknown. In brief, the challenge of ekphrasis is to describe something, via words, for the benefit of those who have not seen it.

A good example of such a text is the essay Goethe wrote in 1817 on Leonardo da Vinci's painting *The Last Supper*. Goethe begins in a style strikingly similar to that of an airline magazine article, first introducing Leonardo da Vinci to his German readers, then going on to inform them that *The Last Supper* is a very famous painting and that Goethe himself actually saw it "several years ago" in Milan. He asks his readers to refer to an engraving of the painting, so that they can better understand his comments, but the tone of his text reflects the pleasure, enthusiasm, and difficulty involved in conveying the experience of viewing a beautiful object to people who have never seen it. Goethe was interested in painting and architecture; he also wrote an ambitious and absurd book about colors. The fact that his literary talent was verbal rather than visual is an ironic contradiction we often encounter in literature—but here I would like to focus on something different.

The creative urge to write novels is motivated by an enthusiasm and a will to express visual things with words. There are, of course, personal, political, and ethical motivations behind every novel, but these could also be satisfied through other media, such as memoirs, interviews, poetry, or journalisms.

When I was growing up in Istanbul in the 1960s, before there was television in Turkey, my brother and I used to listen to soccer games being reported live on the radio. The commentator provided a play-by-play description, transforming what he was seeing into words and making it possible for me and my brother to form a picture of the action taking place in the stadium, whose layout we knew from first-hand experience. He would give precise descriptions of a player's trajectory across the field, the finesse of a passing maneuver, the angle of the ball as it approached the goal on the Bosporus side. Because we listened to the reporter regularly and had grown accustomed to his voice, style, and turn of phrase—just as we did when reading one of our favorite novelists—we were quite good at transforming his words into images, and would feel as if we were practically watching the game. We became addicted to the broadcasts, developing a private, intense relationship with the reporter's voice and language, so that listening to the live coverage would satisfy us almost as much as watching the game in the stadium. The pleasures of writing and reading a novel are much like the pleasures derived from this kind of listening. We get used to it, desire it, and delight in our close relationship with the narrator. We feel the joy of seeing, and of enabling others to see, through words.

I would like to mention the well-known and now largely forgotten example of the "objective correlative," defined by T. S. Eliot in the essay "Hamlet and His Problems." (With regard to my previous lecture, let me note that Eliot says at the beginning of this essay that the psychology—meaning the character—of the hero in a dramatic work is less significant than the effect of the work as a whole.) By "objective correlative," Eliot means "a set of objects, a situation, a chain of events" that will objectively correspond to—that will be the "formula" of, the automatic evocation of—a particular emotion which the artist seeks to express in a poem, painting, novel, or other artwork. We might say that, in the novel, the objective correlative is the picture of the moment that is made with words and that is seen through the eyes of the hero. Eliot actually borrowed the term "objective correlative" from the American Romantic landscape painter Washington Allston (1779–1843). Allston was also a poet, and a friend of Coleridge. Thirty years after Allston, a group of French poets and painters that included Gérard de Nerval, Charles Baudelaire, and Théophile Gautier would declare that the inner, spiritual landscape was the most significant element of poetry and that the essential component in landscape painting was emotion. Coincidentally, two of these writers, Nerval and Gautier, visited Istanbul and wrote about the city and its landscapes.

Tolstoy does not tell us what Anna's feelings are as she rides on the St. Petersburg train. Instead, he paints pictures that help us to feel these emotions: the snow visible from the window on the left, the activity in the compartment, the cold weather, and so on. Tolstoy describes how Anna takes the novel out of her red handbag and how, with her small hands, she places a cushion in her lap. Then he goes on to describe the people in the compartment. And this is precisely when we, as readers, understand that Anna cannot focus her mind on the book, that she has lifted her head from the page, and that she is paying attention to the people in the compartment—and by mentally transforming Tolstoy's words to create the images Anna is seeing, we come to feel her emotions. If we were reading an older form of

literary narrative such as an epic poem, or the sort of
bad novel that presents events and images from the
reader's point of view rather than that of the protagonist, then we would be forgiven for thinking that Anna
is absorbed in reading the novel, but that the narrator
has temporarily set her aside and is describing the compartment in order to add a bit of scenic color. In his essay "Narrate or Describe?" Hungarian critic György
Lukács made a clear distinction between these two
kinds of novelists. In *Anna Karenina,* we follow the action—such as a horse race—through the eyes of Anna,
strongly identifying with her emotions. Whereas in
Zola's *Nana,* when a horse race is depicted, we watch it
from an outside perspective; the encyclopedic description is, said Lukács, "mere filler, hardly an integral element in the action." Whatever the writer's intention
may be, the features that I am calling the "landscape" of
the novel—the objects, words, dialogues, and everything which is visible—should be seen as integral to,
and an extension of, the hero's emotions. This is made
possible by the novel's secret center, which I have mentioned before.

We have now come to what Eliot terms "a set of objects." The landscape I speak of in these lectures is the
landscape of cities, streets, shops, display windows,
rooms, interiors, furniture, and everyday objects,

rather than the type of landscape Stendhal presents in the opening pages of *The Red and the Black*—a small town and its inhabitants, seen from the reader's point of view:

> The little town of Verrières is one of the prettiest in Franche-Comté. Its white houses, with their red-tiled, pointed roofs stretch out along the side of a hill where clumps of chestnut trees thrust sturdily upward at each little bend. Down in the valley the river Doubs flows by, some hundreds of feet below fortifications which were built centuries ago by the Spaniards, but have long since fallen into decay.

It is impossible not to see a connection between the great advances in the art of the novel in the mid-nineteenth century—when it became the dominant literary form in Europe—and the sudden exponential increase in European affluence during the same period, which resulted in a veritable flood of material goods into cities and homes: an abundance and variety of objects unprecedented in the Western world. Especially in urban life, the massive wealth generated by the Industrial Revolution surrounded people with new devices, consumer goods, art objects, clothes, textiles, paintings, trinkets, and bric-à-brac. The newspapers in which these objects were described, the changing lives and tastes of the classes that used them, the countless advertisements, and the various signs and notices in the city landscape became a significant and colorful part of Western culture. All this visual profusion, this surfeit of objects, this hectic urban activity, banished the simpler ways of living which had seemed so straightforward in the good old days. People now felt that they had lost sight of the bigger picture amid the welter of details, and they suspected that meaning was hidden somewhere in the shadows. Adjusting to new modes of life, the modern city-dweller discovered part of the meaning he sought in these life-enriching objects. The place of an individual in society and in novels was determined partly by his home, his possessions, his clothes, his rooms, his furniture, and his bric-à-brac. In his poetic and quite visual novel *Sylvie,* published in 1853, Nerval says that in those days many people collected curios to decorate apartments in old-fashioned buildings.

Balzac was the first writer to incorporate the social and personal appetite for objects and bric-à-brac into the landscape of his novels. Both Stendhal's novel *The Red and the Black* and Balzac's *Père Goriot,* which was written at about the same time, open with an exterior description (that is, from the reader's point of view) of the setting in which the events will take place. In Stendhal, the place we gradually enter is a small, quaint town nestled in a valley, but in Balzac the setting is very different: he gives a detailed portrait of a boarding house, beginning with the wicket gate and the garden. The following descriptions are taken from *Old Goriot*, the translation of Balzac's novel by Marion Ayton Crawford. There are horsehair chairs, a table with a top of Sainte-Anne marble, a white china tea-service whose gilt pattern is half worn away ("the kind of tea-service that is inevitably found everywhere today," Balzac adds scornfully, making his point clearer), vases of artificial flowers imprisoned within bell jars and flanking a vulgar bluish marble clock, food smells lingering in the air, stained decanters, thick blue-bordered earthenware, a barometer, some engravings bad enough to spoil your appetite and framed in varnished black wood with gilt beading, a clock with a tortoiseshell case inlaid with copper, a green stove, lamps coated with dust and oil, a long table covered with oilcloth so greasy that a facetious boarder can write his name on it with his fingernail, broken-backed chairs, sorry-looking rush mats that are always fraying without ever falling apart completely, and shabby foot-warmers, their openings enlarged by decay, their hinges broken, their wood charred. We read these details not only as portraying

the objects in the protagonists' home, but as an extension of the character of Madame Vauquer, who runs
the place ("Her whole person explains the boarding
house, just as the boarding house implies her person").

For Balzac, describing objects and interiors was a way
of allowing the reader to deduce the social status and
psychological makeup of the novel's protagonists, just
as a detective might follow clues to discover the identity
of a criminal. In *L'Education sentimentale,* which
Flaubert (a much subtler novelist) published thirty-five
years after Balzac wrote *Le Père Goriot,* the protagonists become acquainted with and judge one another
by using Balzac's methods—by making note of their
possessions, their clothes, and the bric-à-brac that
adorns their sitting rooms. The following excerpt is
from the translation by Adrianne Tooke: "[Mademoi-
selle Vatnaz] took off her gloves and examined the furniture and the ornaments in the room. . . . She congrat-
ulated [Frédéric] on his good taste. . . . Round her
wrists she wore an edging of lace, and the bodice of her
green dress was braided like a hussar's jacket. Her bon-
net of black tulle, with its drooping brim, concealed her
forehead a little."

As I was voraciously reading Western novels in my
twenties, I often came across descriptions of objects
and clothes that were beyond my limited knowledge of

life—and whenever I was unable to convert these things into mental images, I would refer to dictionaries and encyclopedias. But sometimes even this would not solve the difficulty of transforming the words into pictures in my mind. Then I would try to see these objects as an extension of a mood, and I would relax only when I succeeded.

Let us look at the modern French novel. Material things that, in Balzac, reveal the social status of the hero can serve, in Flaubert, to indicate more subtle qualities, such as personal taste and character. In Zola, they may signal a display of authorial objectivity. Zola is the sort of writer who thinks, "Oh, Anna is reading—so while she does that, let me describe the compartment a bit." The same material things (though perhaps they are no longer the same things) can become, in Proust, a stimulus evoking memories of the past; in Sartre, a symptom of the nausea of existence; and in Robbe-Grillet, mysterious and playful entities independent of human beings. In Georges Perec, objects are dull commodities whose poetry can be seen only if they are considered along with their brands and lined up in series, in lists. All of these views are persuasive, depending on the context. Yet the most important point is that objects are essential parts of the countless discrete moments in novels, as well as the emblems or signs of those moments.

Our minds perform simultaneous tasks when we read a novel. On one hand, we look at the world from the viewpoint of the protagonists, and identify with the characters' emotions. On the other hand, we mentally cluster the objects around the protagonists, and link the details of the described landscape with their emotions. Writing a novel involves combining the emotions and thoughts of each protagonist with the objects that surround him, and then blending them, with a single deft stroke, in one sentence. We do not separate, as the naive novel reader does, the events and objects, the drama and the descriptions. We see them as an integrated whole. The textual approach of the reader who exclaims, "I'm skipping the descriptions!" is of course naive—but the writer who segregates the events from the descriptions has actually stimulated this naive response. Once we have begun to read a novel and have worked our way into it, we do not see a certain type of landscape; on the contrary, we instinctively try to determine where we are in the vast forest of moments and details. But when we encounter the individual trees—that is, the discrete moments and sentences that make up the novel—we want to see not only the events, the flow, and the drama, but also the visual correlative of that moment. The novel thus appears in our mind as a real, three-dimensional, convincing world. Then, rather than perceiving divisions between the events and the objects, the drama and the landscape, we sense an overarching unity, just as in life. When writing a novel, I always feel the need to see the story in my mind frame by frame, and to select or create the *right* frame.

Consider this example from Henry James. In his preface to *The Golden Bowl*, he explains how he decided which minor character he would choose as the viewpoint for his narration (this was always the most important technical problem for James). He uses the expression "seeing my story," and then describes the narrator as a "painter," because the narrator keeps his distance from the action and does not get embroiled in its moral dilemmas. James is a writer who always feels that being a novelist means painting with words. In his prefaces and critical essays, he continually uses terms such as "panorama," "picture," and "painter," in either the literal or the metaphorical sense.

Let us recall Proust's comment, "Mon volume est un tableau" ("My book is a painting," or "My novel is a picture"), referring to the famous work to which he dedicated his life. Toward the end of *A la recherche du temps perdu,* one of the characters, a well-known writer named Bergotte, is lying sick in bed and happens to read in the newspaper that a critic has written about a small patch of yellow wall depicted in Vermeer's *View of*

Delft. The critic says the detail is so beautifully painted that it's comparable to a classical Chinese masterpiece. Bergotte rises from his bed to go to the museum and take another look at Vermeer's painting, which he is convinced he knows very well. Upon seeing the exquisite patch of yellow, he ruefully utters his final words: "That is how I ought to have written. . . . My last books are too dry. I ought to have gone over them with a few layers of color, made my language precious in itself like this little patch of yellow wall." (I quote from the translation by C. K. Scott-Moncrieff and Stephen Hudson.) Like many French novelists who enjoyed putting descriptive passages in their work, Proust took a great interest in painting. Here I feel that he expresses, via his writer-hero Bergotte, a view that closely reflected his own feelings. But let us ask first, with a smile, that inevitable question: "Monsieur Proust, are you Bergotte?"

I have no trouble understanding why the great novelists I admire strove to become like painters, or why they were envious of painting, or why they regretted being unable to write "like a painter." Because the task of writing a novel is to imagine a world—a world that first exists as a picture before it eventually takes the form of words. Only later do we express through words the picture we imagine, so that readers can share this product of the imagination. And since the novelist cannot step back, like Horace's painter, and comfortably survey his work from a distance (for this would require reading the entire novel one more time), he is much more familiar than a painter is with the individual details—the trees rather than the forest, the single moments represented by the objects. A painting is a form of mimesis: it provides us with a representation of reality. When we gaze at a painting, we sense not only the world that the painting belongs to, but also what Heidegger felt when he looked at Van Gogh's masterpiece *A Pair of Shoes:* the thingness of the painting, its status as an object. For the painting has brought us face to face with a representation of the world and the things in it. In a novel, however, we can encounter this world and these things only by converting the writer's descriptions into pictures in our imagination. The Bible declares, "In the beginning was the Word." The art of the novel might say, "In the beginning there seems to be the picture, but it must be told in words." And ironically, the entire history of painting—especially premodern painting, which was mostly illustrative—says, "In the beginning was the word, but it must be told in pictures."

The power and immediacy of images, as opposed to words, explains the secret feelings of inferiority, the deep-seated envy, that novelists—who have an intuitive understanding of the situation—feel toward painters.

But the novelist is not simply someone who wants to become a painter; rather, the novelist seeks the ability to paint with words and descriptions. The novelist feels two parallel obligations: on the one hand, to identify and see the world through the eyes of his protagonists, and, on the other, to describe things with words. Henry James may have called the narrator of *The Golden Bowl* a "painter" for keeping a distance from the action—but to me, the precise opposite is true. The novelist can describe things in the manner of a painter because he is just as interested in the things that surround his characters as he is in the characters themselves, and because he is not outside the world of the novel, but completely immersed in it. The *image juste* that the novelist must find, prior to the Flaubertian *mot juste*, can be discovered only when the writer completely enters the landscape, the events, and the world of the novel. This is also the only way in which the novelist can show the compassion he must feel toward the people he writes about. So we must conclude: the descriptions of things in a novel are (or should be) the outcome and expression of compassion felt for the characters.

Since a part of my identity has its roots in an Islamic culture that does not get on very well with the art of figurative depiction, I will present one or two examples from my own life. In the Istanbul of my childhood, de-

spite the encouragement of the secular state, works of
fine art that would repay extended contemplation and
analysis did not exist. On the other hand, Istanbul cine-
mas would fill to the brim with crowds who took great
pleasure in watching movies, regardless of the nature of
the film being screened. But in movies, just as in
premodern literary narratives and epics, most of the
time we would see the fictional world not from the
point of view of the heroes, but from outside, from
afar. Of course, many of these films came from the
West, from the Christian world—but deep down I
would feel that it was the lack of interest in the art of
painting that lay behind the lack of compassion we felt
for both local and foreign heroes of novels and films.
But I couldn't entirely understand it. Perhaps we feared
that seeing objects and people through other people's
eyes would sever our ties with the beliefs of the community we belonged to. Reading novels served as my
passage from the traditional world to the modern
world. This also meant that I severed my ties with a
community I should have belonged to. I passed, instead, into solitude.

During the same period in my life, when I was
twenty-three, I gave up the dream of becoming a
painter, which I had cherished since I was seven, and

started writing novels. For me, this was a decision related to being happy. As a child, I had been very happy when I painted—but suddenly, and for no discernible reason, this pleasure vanished. Over the next thirty-five years, as I wrote novels, I continued to think that I actually had a far greater and more natural talent for painting. But for a reason I could not make out, I now wanted to paint with words. I have always felt more childlike and naive when I paint, and more adult and sentimental when I write novels. It was as if I wrote novels only with my intellect, and produced paintings solely with my talent. As my hand drew a line or applied the paint, I would look at my hand's work almost in amazement. Not until much later would my mind grasp what was going on. And when writing novels, whenever I am overcome with rapture, it is only much later that I perceive exactly where I stand amid the myriad Nabokovian "nerve endings," the irreducible Aristotelian moments.

From Victor Hugo to August Strindberg, there have been many novelists who also took pleasure in creating paintings. Strindberg, who liked to paint turbulent romantic landscapes, says in his autobiographical novel *The Son of a Servant* that painting made him "indescribably happy—as if he'd just taken hashish." When he experienced this joy of painting for the first time, he was only twenty-three, precisely the same age I was when I quit painting. Both in writing novels and in painting, the supreme goal must be to attain such immense happiness.

5

Museums and Novels

For a long time now, I have been trying to establish a museum in Istanbul. Ten years ago I bought a derelict building in Çukurcuma, a neighborhood close to the studio where I do my writing, and with the help of my architect friends I slowly transformed the structure, built in 1897, into a museum space that looked modern and that reflected my tastes. At the same time, I was also writing a novel, as well as keeping an eye out for items in secondhand shops, flea markets, and the homes of acquaintances who liked to hoard things. I was looking for objects that could have been used by the fictitious family whom I imagined to be living in that old house from 1975 to 1984, and who were the focus of my novel. My studio was gradually filling up with old medicine bottles, bags of buttons, National Lottery tickets, playing cards, clothes, and kitchen utensils.

Intending to use them in my novel, I was imagining situations, moments, and scenes suited to these objects, many of which (such as a quince grater) I had bought on impulse. Once, when browsing in a secondhand shop, I found a dress in a bright fabric with orange roses and green leaves on it, and I decided it was just right for Füsun, the heroine of my novel. With the dress laid out before me, I proceeded to write the details of a scene in which Füsun is learning to drive while wearing that very dress. On another occasion, in an antiquarian bookshop in Istanbul, I spotted a black-and-white photo from the 1930s. I imagined it showed a scene from the early life of one of my characters, and I decided to channel my story through the objects it depicted, even to insert descriptions of the photo itself. Furthermore, as I'd done in several of my other novels, I planned to give my characters many of my own attributes, or those of my mother, father, and relatives—so I would choose various objects that belonged to family members, and that I loved and remembered, and I would place these in front of me. I would describe them in detail, make them part of my story.

This is how I wrote my novel *The Museum of Innocence*—by finding, studying, and describing objects that inspired me. Or sometimes by doing precisely the opposite: trolling the shops for objects that the novel required, or having them made to order by artists and craftsmen. By the time the novel was finished, in 2008, both my studio and my home were piled high with objects. And I became determined to establish a real-life

version of the Museum of Innocence described in the
novel. But this museum is not my topic right now. Neither is the idea of constructing a novel by collecting the
objects mentioned in the story or by using memories
related to these objects as points of departure. I would
like to focus on the reasons one might have for associating real objects—paintings, photographs, items of
clothing—with a novel. My first observation concerns
the jealousy of novelists: their half-secret, perhaps un-
conscious envy of painters that I mentioned earlier
when talking about pictures and objects. In contrast to
what Heidegger called the "thingness" of a work of art,
what I am talking about is the feeling of insufficiency
one gets when reading novels—a feeling born of the
fact that novels need the willing participation of the
reader's imagination.

Let us try to describe the insufficiency we feel when
we read a novel, when we think via the medium of a
novel. As we get further and further into the story, as
we joyfully lose our way in the forest of details and in-
cidents, its world seems far more substantial to us than
real life. One reason for this is the relationship between
the secret center of the novel and the most basic aspects
of life—a relationship that empowers novels to provide
a greater feeling of authenticity than life itself. Another
reason is that novels are built with everyday, universal,

human sensations. Yet another reason is that in novels—and this is generally also true of genre novels, such as crime fiction, romances, science fiction, and erotic novels—we find the sensations and experiences that are missing in our own life.

Whatever the reason may be, the sounds, smells, and images of the world we encounter in novels evoke a sensation of authenticity we fail to find in life itself. But on the other hand, novels put nothing concrete in front of us—not a single object to touch, not a smell, not a sound, not a taste. When we're reading a good novel, a part of our mind thinks we are immersed in reality—indeed, at a profoundly deep point in that reality—and that life is exactly like this experience. Meanwhile, though, our senses are reporting that this isn't happening at all. This paradoxical situation is what leaves us feeling unsatisfied.

The more powerful and persuasive the novel we are reading, the more painful the feeling of insufficiency. The more the naive side of our soul has believed in and been enthralled by the novel, the more heartbreaking our disappointment at having to accept the fact that the world it describes is merely imaginary. In order to relieve this particular frustration, novel readers want to validate the fictional world with their own senses, even though they know that much of what they are reading has originated in the writer's imagination. They're just like my professor friend who was extremely well-versed in literary theory and the nature of fiction, but who *still* forgot that I wasn't my novel's hero, Kemal.

When I first went to Paris at the age of thirty, having read all the major French novels, I rushed to places I had encountered in their pages. I went, like Balzac's hero Rastignac, to look down on Paris from the heights of Père Lachaise Cemetery, and was surprised to discover how ordinary it all was. Yet in my first novel, *Cevdet Bey and Sons*, I had created a hero who explicitly takes Rastignac as his role model. In the twentieth century, the major cities of Europe that served as the stage for the art of the novel became full of aspiring non-Western writers who had learned about the world through the medium of the novel and wanted to believe that what they had learned was more than a figment of the imagination. It is common knowledge that there are novel-lovers who tour Spain with a copy of *Don Quixote* in hand. The irony, of course, is that Cervantes's hero is himself mixed up, confusing chivalric literature with reality. The most extraordinary example of an intellect caught between fiction and reality was Vladimir Nabokov, who once said that all novels were fairy tales but who tried to compile an annotated edition of *Anna Karenina* that would reveal the "facts" behind the novel.

Although he never completed the project, he researched and drew the layout of the railway car that Anna traveled in from Moscow to St. Petersburg. He carefully noted the plainness of the compartment reserved for women, which seats were allotted to the poorer passengers, the location of the heating stove, what the windows looked like, and the distance in miles from Moscow to St. Petersburg—all the information that Tolstoy neglected to include. I don't think that such annotations contribute much toward our understanding of the novel or of Anna's thoughts, but we take pleasure in reading them. They lead us to think that Anna's story is real, to believe in her even more, and, just for a moment, to forget our feelings of disappointment and insufficiency.

Our efforts as readers include an important element of vanity, which I would now like to touch on. I have already said that when we read a novel, we do not encounter anything real, as we do when we look at a painting, and that it's actually we ourselves who bring the world of the novel into existence by transforming words into mental images and employing our imagination. Every reader will remember a particular novel in his own unique way, with his own unique images. Of course, when it comes to using the imagination, some readers are rather lazy while others are quite diligent. A writer who caters to lazy imaginations will explicitly convey the feelings and thoughts that readers should feel when a particular image appears in the mind's eye. Whereas the novelist who trusts in the reader's power of imagination will merely describe and define with words the images that constitute the moments of the novel, and will leave the feelings and thoughts up to the reader. Sometimes—in fact, often—our imagination fails to form a picture or any corresponding feeling, and we end up telling ourselves that we "didn't understand the novel." Often, though, we work hard to set our imagination in motion, and make a real effort to visualize the images that the writer has suggested or that the text wants to create in our mind. And because of our efforts to understand and to visualize, a certain proud possessiveness toward the novel slowly arises within us. We begin to feel that the novel was written just for us, and that it is only we who truly understand it.

This feeling of possessiveness also stems from the fact that we, the readers, are the ones who bring the novel into existence, by picturing it in our mind's eye. The novelist, after all, needs diligent, tolerant, perceptive readers like us to complete the realization of the novel, to make the novel "work." And in order to prove we are this special kind of reader, we pretend to forget that the novel is a product of the imagination. And we want to visit the cities, streets, and houses where the events take place. Contained within this desire is the urge to better understand the world of the novel and, in equal measure, to see that everything is "exactly as we imagined." Seeing *l'image juste*—evoked by the novelist using *le mot juste*—in real streets, homes, and objects not only helps to alleviate the feeling of insufficiency we get from the novel, but also fills us readers with the pride of having imagined the details accurately.

This kind of pride and its variations are the shared feelings that link novels and museums, or novel readers and museum visitors. Our topic here is not museums but novels. Yet in order to illustrate the motives that spark our imagination when we read a novel, I will continue with this example of pride and the museum. Remember that just like chess players who anticipate their opponent's next move, novelists always take into account the reader's imagination and the desires and motives that animate it. How the reader's mind is likely to respond is one of the most important considerations for the novelist.

The complex subject of museums and novels will be easier to discuss if we separate it into three parts. But let's keep in mind that the three parts are interrelated, and that pride is their common element.

1. Self-Regard

The origins of the contemporary museum lie in the *Wunderkammern*—the "cabinets of curiosities"—of the rich and powerful, who, beginning in the seventeenth century, flaunted their wealth by exhibiting seashells, mineral samples, plants, ivory, animal specimens, and paintings from faraway lands and unusual sources. In this sense, the first museums were the grandest rooms and halls of the palaces of European princes and kings —spaces in which the rulers displayed their power, taste, and sophistication through the medium of objects and paintings. Little of the symbolism changed when this ruling elite fell from power, and palaces such as the Louvre were transformed into public museums. The Louvre came to represent not the wealth of the French kings, but the power, culture, and taste of all French citizens. Rare paintings and artifacts were now made accessible to the gaze of average people. We could draw a loose analogy between the development of museums and the historical transition in literary genres: the process by which epics and romances about the adventures of kings and knights gave way to novels, which deal with the life of the middle classes. Yet the real point I wish to make here concerns not the symbolic and representational power of museums and novels, but their archival quality.

We have already noted that novels gain their evocative power by drawing on our everyday experiences and sensations, by capturing the essential features of life. Novels also form a rich and powerful archive—of common human feelings, our perceptions of ordinary things, our gestures, utterances, and attitudes. Various sounds, words, colloquialisms, smells, images, tastes, objects, and colors are remembered only because novelists observe them and carefully make note of them in their writings. When we stand before an object or a painting in a museum, we can only guess, with the help of the catalogue, how the piece fitted into people's lives, stories, and worldviews—while in a novel, the images, objects, conversations, smells, stories, beliefs, and sensations are described and preserved as an integral part of the daily life of the period.

This archival quality of novels, their capacity for preserving customs, attitudes, and ways of living, is especially relevant when it comes to recording casual, everyday speech. Marguerite Yourcenar, in her brilliant essay "Tone and Language in the Historical Novel," tells us which books, writers, and memoirs she read in order to find her narrative voice, and describes how she created the atmosphere in her renowned historical novels *Memoirs of Hadrian* and *The Abyss*. She begins her discussion by reminding readers that, until the invention of the phonograph in the nineteenth century, the voices of prior generations were irretrievably lost. The words and sounds of the millions of people who had lived during thousands of years of history simply vanished. In the same way, prior to the great novelists and playwrights of the nineteenth century, there had been no writer to record people's everyday conversations, with all their spontaneity, disjointed logic, and complexities. Yourcenar highlights an important function of the novel: it incorporates ordinary expressions which are taken directly from life and unaltered by stylistic editing—phrases such as "Please pass the beans," "Who left the door open?" and "Better look out, it's going to rain."

If the core defining quality of a novel is the way it highlights everyday observations, and then recomposes them through the medium of the imagination in order to reveal life's deeper meanings, then Yourcenar's remarks should lead us to conclude that only in the nineteenth century was the art of the novel perfected as we know it today. It is difficult to imagine a novel without the power and persuasiveness of ordinary speech, because everyday language is the natural conduit for those prosaic moments and random sensations on which the world of the novel is based. Of course, such casual dialogues do not necessarily have to be recorded in detail and spaced out on the page, one statement per paragraph, nor is there any need to allow them to dominate the landscape of the novel. This, among many other things, is one of the important lessons to be learned from Proust.

Just as museums preserve objects, novels preserve the nuances, tones, and colors of language, expressing in colloquial terms people's ordinary thoughts and the haphazard way in which the mind skips from one topic to the next. Novels not only preserve words, verbal formulas, and idioms, but they also record how they are used in daily exchanges. When we read James Joyce, we discover the same wordplay and linguistic inventiveness that delight us when we hear a child learning to speak. After Joyce, all the great novelists who played with variations on the interior monologue—from Faulkner to Woolf, from Broch to García Márquez—were less convincing than he had been about the way our minds work, but much more entertaining and observant when it came to the charm and peculiarities of the way language affects our lives.

The capturing of everyday language is a defining fea-

ture of prose fiction, and in this respect the first Turkish novel (identifying the "first" novel in any culture is
always a topic of widespread and heated debate) is
Recaizade Mahmut Ekrem's *A Carriage Affair,* published in 1896. With its focus on Westernization, on the
dangers of Western idolatry, and on the pretentiousness
of pro-Western intellectuals, this novel is one of the
earliest examples of that Ottoman-Turkish creation
known as the "East-West novel," a genre still in use today. (My own *White Castle* is a small contribution to
the tradition of the East-West novel.) *A Carriage Affair*
can be hilarious and brilliant in its portrayal of late
nineteenth-century Ottoman intellectuals—their desire
to imitate the West, and their resulting "tragicomic
confusion" (as the critic Jale Parla phrased it), sometimes rendered in a barely understandable mélange of
Turkish and French. The same artificiality is depicted
by Tolstoy in *War and Peace* when he reproduces the
conversational style of the Russian elite, who on the
one hand are waging war against Napoleon while on
the other are speaking French in their everyday life.
But *A Carriage Affair* does not have the ambitious
structure and profound depth of *War and Peace;* it is
merely a realist satire. The secret center of the novel—
which we constantly and thoughtfully search for with a
corner of our mind while reading Tolstoy, George Eliot,

and Thomas Mann (or, in the past several decades, the best works of V. S. Naipaul, Milan Kundera, J. M. Coetzee, and Peter Handke)—never attracts our curiosity in Ekrem. The first time I read this strange and unique novel, I felt the joy of suddenly finding myself in the mind of an Ottoman intellectual and immersed in the everyday language of 1890s Istanbul. Sadly, such lively depictions and such creative use of colloquialisms, one of the greatest pleasures of writing a novel, is often lost when the prose is translated into other languages.

The fact that, as Yourcenar says, everyday utterances were not recorded prior to the emergence of the novel should remind us of the absurdity—the impossibility— of what is known as the "historical novel." When refer- ring to the "fatal cheapness" of historical novels and the naïveté of their readers, Henry James was talking not only about words, but also about the difficulties of pen- etrating the consciousness of a different time. When I was writing my own historical novel *My Name Is Red,* I was aware that meticulously reading Ottoman court registers, business records, and public documents to find details of everyday life would not suffice to over- come this gap in comprehension. I decided to reveal and exaggerate the contrived aspect of the narrative, and thereby to avoid concocting false renderings of sixteenth-century Istanbul conversation, something we

know nothing about. Every now and then, my protagonists will look out from the page and directly address
the reader. I also endowed certain objects and paintings
with the ability to speak. And I included numerous ref-
erences to the contemporary world—in fact, the daily
life of the family in the novel is based on my life with
my mother and brother.

From the 1980s on, innovations that can generally be
described as "postmodernist" emerged in the world
novel, beginning with the influence of writers like Jorge
Luis Borges and Italo Calvino, who were essentially re-
searchers into the metaphysics of fiction, rather than
novelists in the strict sense of the word. Their work
enhanced the authenticity and persuasiveness of the
novel—topics that occupied Yourcenar as much as
Henry James—and consolidated the tradition of thinking via the medium of the novel.

But the museum-like quality of novels that I wish to
dwell on is less about provoking thought and more
about preservation, conservation, and the resistance to
being forgotten. Just like families who go to a museum
on Sundays, thinking that it preserves something of
their own past and deriving pleasure from this thought,
readers, too, take great pleasure in finding that a novel
incorporates facets of their actual life—the bus stop at
the end of their street, the newspaper they read, the

film they love, the view of the evening sun they see from their window, the tea they drink, the posters and advertisements they see, the alleyways, boulevards, and squares they walk along, and—as I witnessed after *The Black Book* was published in Istanbul—even the stores they go to (like Aladdin's shop). The reason for this happiness perhaps parallels the illusion and subsequent pride we feel in museums: the feeling that history is not hollow and meaningless, and that something from the life we live will be preserved. The popular and empty belief in the immortality of novels and poetry—one that sometimes also overcomes me—merely serves to strengthen this pride and this consolation. The pleasure the novel-reader gains is different from that of the museum visitor because, rather than preserving objects themselves, novels preserve our encounters with those objects—that is, our perception of them.

Like many other novelists, I have often heard people say, "Mr. Pamuk, this is exactly what I saw, and exactly what I felt. It's as though you've written about my own life!" I have never known whether to feel happy or sad at hearing these well-intentioned words. Because whenever I hear them I feel less like a creative novelist who produces stories out of nothing by using his imagination, and more like a chronicler who simply records the life we share as a community, with all its phrases, images, and objects. I think this is an honorable and pleasing occupation. But those well-intentioned words of the gentle reader give me the impression that—as communities, images, and objects mutate and disperse with the passage of time, with historical change, and with death—novels will be forgotten as well. And indeed, this is generally the case. The topic of the permanence of novels and the immortality of writers is, as you can see, firmly rooted in human vanity.

2. The Sense of Distinction

The French sociologist Pierre Bourdieu has written extensively on the topic of distinction, in a social context. He explores, among other facets, the feeling of distinction that art-lovers experience when they take pleasure in works of art. Some of Bourdieu's observations relate to museums and museum visitors, but I would like to apply his ideas to novelists and novel-readers.

Let me begin with a story that was popular among Istanbul intellectuals a decade ago. After two partial translations of Proust were published in the 1940s and the 1960s, Roza Hakmen translated Proust's entire seven-volume work into Turkish in the years 1996–2002. She made effective use of the Turkish language's affinity for long sentences, as well as its other subtleties, and the majority of Istanbul newspapers applauded her rendering as extremely successful. Much was said about Proust on the radio, on TV, and in the press, and the first few volumes of the novel even appeared on the bestseller lists. Around that time, at Istanbul Technical University a large number of new students lined up to enroll at the start of the school year. The story goes that a girl waiting somewhere at the back of the line—let's call her Ayşe—took from her handbag, not without a certain prideful flourish, a volume of *Kayıp Zamanın İzinde* (In Search of Lost Time) and began to read. Every now and then she would lift her head from the book to gaze at the students she would be spending the next four years with. In particular, she noticed a girl standing a little further ahead—let's call her Zeynep— who was wearing high-heeled shoes, too much makeup, and a tasteless, expensive dress. With a scornful smile at Zeynep's superficial airs, Ayşe would tighten her grasp on her Proust. A little while later, however, lifting her head from the book, Ayşe was dismayed to see Zeynep remove from her handbag and begin to read the very same volume. Thinking it was inconceivable that she could be reading the same novel as a girl who looked like Zeynep, she lost all interest in Proust.

While showing us that a girl like Ayşe visits museums partly to prove that she is not like Zeynep, Bourdieu also reveals that such decisions are influenced by a fair amount of class and community consciousness. The same factors apply, as our story shows, when it comes to reading novels—but that experience entails more individuality and a more deeply personal aspect that I want to stress here. I have already said that when we read a novel we often feel that the writer is addressing us alone, since we have made such an effort to visualize the writer's words and see the images the writer has presented in written form. Eventually, we come to love certain novels because we have expended so much imaginative labor on them. This is why we hang on to those novels, whose pages are creased and dog-eared. In the 1980s, as large-scale tourism was just beginning in Istanbul, whenever I went to a secondhand bookstore that sold volumes left behind in hotel rooms by tourists, I rarely found novels I wanted to read—the offerings were mostly garish paperbacks—and I sensed that the books people cast off were only the ones they had been able to read without making an effort.

The effort we invest in reading and visualizing a novel is connected with our desire to be special and to set ourselves apart from other people. And this feeling links up with our desire to identify with the novel's characters, whose lives are different from ours. When reading *Ulysses*, we feel good, first of all, because we try to identify with the characters, whose lives, dreams, surroundings, fears, plans, and traditions are so different from our own. But then this feeling is augmented by our awareness that we are reading a "difficult" novel —and somewhere in the back of our mind, we feel we are engaging in an activity of a certain distinction. As we read the work of a challenging writer like Joyce, part of our brain is busy congratulating ourselves for reading a writer like Joyce.

When Ayşe took her volume of Proust out of her handbag on registration day, she was intending not to waste the time she spent standing in line; but she probably also wanted to show how different she was, making a social gesture that would enable her to find other students who were like her. We could describe Ayşe as a sentimental-reflective reader who was well aware of the meaning of her gesture. And it's likely that Zeynep was the naive kind of reader who, compared to Ayşe, was less conscious of the air of distinction that novels can confer upon their readers. At least we can assume, without risk of being mistaken, that she appeared this way to Ayşe. The reader's naïveté and sentimentality are— like an awareness of the novel's artifice—related to an interest in the context and manner in which the novel is read, and the place of the writer in this context.

By way of contrast, recall that Dostoyevsky wrote *The*

Devils, the greatest political novel of all time, as a work
of propaganda aimed at his political opponents, Russia's Westernizers and liberals—yet the element in it
that gives readers the greatest pleasure today is its profound portrayal of human nature. The context in which
novels are written is unimportant, nor does it matter
where they are read. The only thing that matters is what
the text tells us. The desire to immerse oneself in the
text is akin to the desire of the museum visitor who
wants to be left alone with the timeless beauty of a
painting, regardless of whatever corporation or government is using the museum for propaganda purposes.
(Thomas Bernhard wrote a novel entitled *Old Masters*
that subtly plays on this desire.) But it is impossible to
speak of the "timeless" beauty of novels, because they
can be completed and realized only within the imagination of the reader, who lives in Aristotelian Time. When
we look at a painting, we immediately grasp its general
composition—but in a novel, we must gradually tra-
verse a great forest by forming each and every tree in
our imagination, so we can arrive at the overall composition and attain that "timeless" beauty. Without knowing from the outset the writer's intentions, the problems of his culture, the novel's details and images, and
the kind of reader the novel addresses, we cannot
achieve such visualization and transform words into

pictures. The art of the novel as we know it today, which was developed in the mid-nineteenth century by Balzac, Stendhal, and Dickens—let's give it its due and call it the "great nineteenth-century novel"—is only a hundred and fifty years old. I have no doubt that those superb writers will live forever in the hearts of today's French- and English-speaking readers like immortal symbols, emblems of language. But I am not sure whether, a hundred and fifty years from now, the generations of the future will appreciate them as much.

The reader's intentions are just as important as those of the writer, when it comes to the completion and realization of a novel. I am, of course, a reader as well as a writer. Just like Ayşe, I enjoy reading a novel that no one else seems interested in—enjoy the feeling that I've discovered it myself. And like many readers, I'm fond of imagining the novel's author as being unhappy and misunderstood. At such a moment, I feel that I'm the only one who understands the most neglected corners of that neglected novel. I am filled with pride because I identify with the characters, and at the same time feel as though the author himself is personally whispering the novel in my ear. The epitome of this pride comes when the reader feels as if he has written the work himself. I wrote about such a reader, an ardent admirer of Proust, in the chapter entitled "Love Stories on a Snowy

Evening" in *The Black Book*. (I might add that I also like
going to museums no one goes to, and that—just like
Kemal, the hero of *The Museum of Innocence*—I find a
certain poetry of Time and Space in empty museums,
where the guards doze and the parquet flooring creaks.)
Reading a novel that no one else knows makes us feel
that we are doing the writer a favor, so we redouble our
efforts and exert our imagination that much more
while reading the book.

The hard part of understanding a novel is not figur-
ing out the intentions of the writer and the responses
of the reader, but achieving a balanced view of this information and determining what the text is trying to
relate. Remember that the novelist writes his text by
constantly making guesses about the likely interpreta-
tions of the reader, and that the reader reads the novel
guessing that the writer has written the novel while
making such guesses. Novelists also figure that readers
will read their novels believing themselves to be the
writer, or imagining the writer as an unhappy and neglected person, and they write accordingly. Perhaps I'm
revealing too many trade secrets here—my member-
ship in the guild might be revoked!

Some novelists are determined to avoid even beginning this real or imagined chess game with their readers, while others play this game to the very end. Some

novelists write to erect a great monument in the eyes of the reader (in one of his early essays, a review of *Ulysses*, Borges likens Joyce's book to a cathedral; and Proust considered titling the volumes of his novel after the various parts of a cathedral). Some novelists take pride in understanding others; some take pride in *not* being understood by others. These contrasting aims suit the nature of the novel. On the one hand, writers try to understand others, to identify with and feel compassion for others, while on the other hand they try, in a masterful and subtle way, to both conceal and suggest the novel's center—its deeper meaning, a single comprehensive view of the forest from a distance. The central paradox of the art of the novel is the way the novelist strives to express his own personal worldview while also seeing the world through the eyes of others.

3. Politics

It has become commonplace to talk about politics when talking about museums. On the other hand, talking about politics in a novel, or talking politics when talking about novels, is done less frequently today, especially in the West. In *The Charterhouse of Parma*, Stendhal compares such talk to a gunshot in the middle of a concert—something vulgar, but impossible to ignore. Perhaps this is because the novel, now a hundred and fifty years old, has matured in late childhood, whereas museums had a more difficult coming of age. I am not complaining. The political novel is a limited genre because politics entails a determination not to understand those who are different from us, while the art of the novelist entails a determination to understand those who are different from us. But the extent to which politics can be included in novels is boundless, because the novelist becomes political in the very effort to understand those who are different from him, those who belong to other communities, races, cultures, classes, and nations. The most political novel is the novel that has no political themes or motives but that tries to see everything and understand everyone, to construct the largest whole. Thus, the novel that manages to accomplish this impossible task has the deepest center.

We visit a museum; we look at some paintings and artifacts; and then, over the weekend, we read the review of the exhibition in the newspaper, speculating on the politics behind the curator's choices. Why was one painting chosen over another? Why were other works sidelined? The trouble that afflicts both museums and novels, and thus creates a kinship between them, is the problem of representation and its political consequences. This problem is more apparent in relatively poor non-Western countries, where the readership is smaller.

Let me take us into this subject by mentioning a reverse example and a personal prejudice. Compared to writers in other countries, novelists in the United States write nearly effortlessly when it comes to social and political constraints. They take for granted the wealth and education of an established literary audience, feel little conflict over whom and what to portray, and—often a damning side-effect of this state of affairs—experience no anxiety about whom they write for, to what end, and why. Though my emotions in this respect are not as strong as Schiller's envy of Goethe's naïveté, I do envy American novelists for their lack of constraint, for the confidence and ease with which they write—in short, for their naïveté. And here is my personal prejudice: I believe this naïveté stems from the recognition shared by writers and readers that they belong to the same class and community, and from the fact that Western writers write not to represent anyone but simply for their own satisfaction.

In contrast, throughout the poorer, non-Western parts of the world (including my homeland, Turkey), the issue of whom and what to represent can be a nightmare for literature and for novelists. The obvious reason is that writers in poor non-Western countries often come from the upper classes. Their use of the Western genre known as the novel, their cultural affiliation and engagement with a different segment of society, and their relatively limited audience are factors that exacerbate the problem. This is why, when it comes to the interpretation and reception of their works, novelists show an acute sensitivity far beyond the pride that is an inherent characteristic of every novelist, and they react in various ways. In my thirty-five years as a novelist living in Turkey, I have encountered every single one of these attitudes, ranging from extreme pride to extreme self-abnegation. And I feel that these reactions are not unique to Turkey—that they stem from the inevitable spiritual wounds sustained by novelists in non-Western countries, where the readership is comparatively small.

The first of these reactions is often an attitude of extreme condescension toward the reader—who is never seen, never taken into account—and an actual pride in the fact that one's novels are not read. Such novelists shield themselves with modernist literary tenets and achieve success not by identifying with others, but by portraying their own world. Nationalists, communitarians, and moralists then put these novelists in their place by letting them know that they are at odds with the prevailing culture.

The second type of novelist struggles to become part

of the community, of the nation. The desire to be liked, the thrill of offering social critique, and the satisfaction of moralizing give these novelists the energy and power to write, the pleasure of producing descriptions, and the determination to observe everything. Such writers who take pride in belonging and representing are, compared to the first type, more successful at creating "a mirror being carried along a road" ("un miroir qu'on promène le long d'un chemin")—which is the metaphor that Stendhal used to describe the novel.

I have simplified here, so as to provide a bird's-eye view. The reality is, of course, far more detailed and complex. Let me tell you a story about myself, to highlight the tangled and contradictory nature of the problem.

I made many visits to the city of Kars in northeast Turkey in preparation for writing *Snow,* which is, on the surface, the most political of all my novels. Because the good-hearted people of Kars knew that I would be writing about them, they never failed to answer, willingly and forthrightly, each and every question I asked. Many of my queries were about poverty, corruption, fraudulent dealings, bribery, and squalor—the town had many social and political problems, with grudges and resentments that often led to violence. Everyone would tell me who the bad guys were and demand that

I write about them. I would spend days going around the streets with a microphone, recording terrible stories about the city and the lives of its residents. Then my friends would take me to the bus station and each time would say goodbye with the same words: "Mr. Pamuk, now please don't write anything negative about us or about Kars, all right?" They would see me off with a smile that hadn't a trace of irony—and I would lose myself in thought, like every novelist who is caught between the urge to write the truth and the desire to be loved.

I used to feel that the way out of this dilemma was to cultivate the type of naïveté that Schiller had observed in Goethe and that I, as a result of my prejudices, attributed to American novelists. But I was also aware of how difficult it was to maintain this naïveté while living among people drowning in a sea of troubles so immense that they had made these harrowing experiences a part of their identity and had come to embrace them. At a certain point I realized that I would not be able to write about Kars just for my own satisfaction. Now, years later, I find myself thinking that perhaps it is because I can no longer write solely for pleasure that I am creating a museum purely for my own happiness.

The Center

The center of a novel is a profound opinion or insight about life, a deeply embedded point of mystery, whether real or imagined. Novelists write in order to investigate this locus, to discover its implications, and we are aware that novels are read in the same spirit. When we first imagine a novel, we may consciously think of this secret center and know that we are writing for its sake—but sometimes we may be unaware of it. At times, a real-life adventure, or a truth about the world learned through first-hand experience, may seem much more important than this center. There are other times when a personal impulse, or the desire to give moral and aesthetic representation to other lives, people, groups, and communities, seems so important that we prefer to ignore the fact that we are writing for the sake of this center. The violence, beauty, novelty, and unexpectedness of the events we relate may even make us forget that the novel we are writing has a center at all. Novelists—some of us only occasionally, others more often—move instinctively, excitedly, and relentlessly from one detail, observation, object, and image to the next, in order to reach the end of the story, giving little thought to the fact that the novel we are writing has a secret center. Writing a novel may resemble traversing a forest, devoting passionate attention to every tree, registering and describing every detail, as though the point were merely to tell the story, to make it through the entire forest.

But however much we are attracted by the woods, buildings, and rivers of the landscape, or find ourselves enchanted by the wonder, strangeness, and beauty of each tree or cliff, we still know that there is something more mysterious locked within the landscape—something more profoundly meaningful than the sum of all the individual trees and the objects it contains. On occasion we may feel this clearly, and sometimes the awareness is accompanied by a haunting sense of disquiet.

The same goes for readers of novels. The reader of the literary novel knows that each tree in the landscape—each person, object, event, anecdote, image, recollection, bit of information, and leap in time—has been placed there to point to the deeper meaning, the secret center that lies somewhere beneath the surface. The novelist may have included some adventures and details because he has actually experienced them, or because he came across them in real life and was attracted by them, or simply because he was able to imagine them so beautifully. But the literary reader knows that all these components that exert their effect by virtue of their beauty, power, and lifelikeness have to feature in the novel because they indicate a secret center, and the reader searches for this center while proceeding through the book.

The writer, too, recognizes the center of the novel as the intuition, thought, or knowledge that inspires the work. But novelists also know that, during the process of writing, this inspiration changes direction and shape. Often the center emerges as the novel is written. Many novelists, at the outset, perceive the center as just a subject, an idea to be conveyed in the form of a story, and they know that they will discover and reveal the deeper meaning of the inevitable and ambiguous center as they develop their novel. As the writing progresses, not only the individual trees but the intermingling branches and leaves of the trees are carefully delineated. The writer's notion of the secret center begins to change, just as the reader's idea of it changes in the course of reading. Reading a novel is the act of determining the real center and the real subject, while also deriving pleasure from the surface details. Exploring the center—in other words, the real subject of the novel—can come to seem much more important than those details.

For example, in a foreword he wrote for Melville's *Bartleby the Scrivener,* Borges describes how the reader gradually reaches the heart of *Moby-Dick.* "At the beginning, the reader might consider the subject to be the arduous life of whale hunters." Indeed, the opening chapters of *Moby-Dick* are like a novel of social criticism, or even newspaper reportage, full of details about whaling and about the lives of the harpooners. "But then," says Borges, we come to think "the subject is the madness of Captain Ahab bent on pursuing and destroying the white whale." And in fact the middle chapters of *Moby-Dick* are like a psychological novel, analyzing the unique character of a powerful man filled with obsessive rage. Finally, Borges reminds us that the real subject and center are something entirely different: "Page by page, the story grows until it takes on the dimensions of the cosmos."

It is a sign of the brilliance and depth of a novel when there is such a distance between the narrated story and its center. *Moby-Dick* is one of those masterpieces in which we constantly feel the presence of the center, constantly ask where it might be, constantly change our mind as to the answer. If one reason for this is the richness of its landscape and the complexity of its characters, another reason is the fact that even the greatest novelists—the most disciplined craftsmen, the most meticulous planners—keep refining their ideas about the center of their novels during the process of writing.

The novelist finds an abundance of material in the details of his own life and in his imagination. He writes in order to explore, develop, and engage deeply with this material. The profound view of life that the novelist wishes to convey in his novel—the insight that I am calling the center—emerges from the details, the overall shape, and the characters, all of which develop as the novel is written. I have taken issue with E. M. Forster's idea—the popular notion that, as the novel is being written, the major characters take over and dictate its course. But if we must believe in a mysterious element in the writing process, it would be more appropriate to believe that it is the *center* that takes over the novel. Just as the sentimental-reflective reader goes through the novel trying to guess exactly where the center is, the experienced novelist goes along knowing that the center will gradually emerge as he writes, and that the most challenging and rewarding aspect of his work will be finding this center and bringing it into focus.

As he constructs the novel and asks himself where its center lies, the novelist begins to sense that the work might have an overall meaning completely at odds with his intentions. An example comes from Dostoyevsky. In July 1870, a year after he had begun planning and writing *The Devils,* Dostoyevsky suffered a series of epileptic attacks. He described the consequences of these attacks in a letter written the following month to his niece, Sofya Ivanova: "Getting back to work, I suddenly saw all at once what the trouble was, and where I had made a mistake—and with this, as if by itself and through inspiration, a new plan appeared in all its proportions. Everything had to be radically changed. Not hesitating for a moment, I struck out everything I had written and began again on page one. The work of an entire year was wiped out."

In *The Miraculous Years,* the fourth volume of a superb biography of Dostoyevsky, Joseph Frank warns the reader that the Russian novelist was exaggerating, as usual. It *was* thanks to this new plan that Dostoyevsky had made the change that would transform his novel from a story about one-dimensional cardboard characters into a brilliant political novel, but in fact he had revised only a fraction of it: forty pages of the two hundred forty pages he had written in the previous year.

Many things remained the same in the novel, including its subject and most of its text. What *had* changed was, yes, the center of the novel.

This locus that I am calling the center, and that we novelists instinctively sense, is so important that even imagining we have changed it gives us the feeling that every sentence and every page of our novel have changed and acquired an entirely different meaning. The center of the novel is like a light whose source remains ambiguous but which nonetheless illuminates the whole forest—every tree, every path, the clearings we have left behind, the glades we are heading toward, the thorny bushes, and the darkest, most impenetrable undergrowth. Only so long as we feel its presence can we proceed. For example, in the preface to his autobiographical work *Finding the Center,* V. S. Naipaul points out how his "narrative ran into the sands" because "it had no center." Even if we are in darkness, we press on with the hope that we will soon see this light.

Both writing and reading a novel require us to integrate all the material that comes from life and from our imagination—the subject, the story, the protagonists, and the details of our personal world—with this light and this center. The ambiguity of their location is never a bad thing; on the contrary, it is a quality we readers demand, for if the center is too obvious and the light too strong, the meaning of the novel is immediately revealed and the act of reading feels repetitive. Reading genre novels—science fiction, crime novels, period fantasies, romance novels—we never ask ourselves the questions Borges asked while reading *Moby-Dick:* What is the real subject? Where is the center? The center of these novels is precisely where we found it before, while reading novels of the same type. Only the adventures, the scenery, the main characters, and the murderers are different. In the genre novel, the profound theme that the narrative must structurally imply remains the same from one book to the next. Apart from the works of a few creative writers like Stanislaw Lem and Philip K. Dick in science fiction, Patricia Highsmith in thrillers and murder mysteries, and John Le Carré in espionage fiction, genre novels do not inspire us with any urge to seek the center at all. It is for this reason that writers of such novels add a new element of suspense and intrigue to their story every few pages. On the other hand, because we are not drained by the constant effort of asking basic questions about the meaning of life, we feel comfortable and safe when reading genre novels.

In fact, the reason we read such novels is to feel the peace and security of being at home, where everything is familiar and in its accustomed place. The reason we turn to literary novels, great novels, where we search for guidance and wisdom that might confer meaning on life, is that we fail to feel at home in the world. To make this claim is to establish, as Schiller does, a relationship between a psychological state and a literary form. Modern man reads and needs novels in order to feel at home in the world, because his relationship to the universe he lives in has been damaged—and in this sense, he has made the transition from naïveté to sentimentality. For psychological reasons, when I was young I felt a strong need to read novels, as well as works of metaphysics, philosophy, and religion. I'll never forget the novels I read in my twenties, feverishly seeking their centers as if this were a matter of life and death. Not only because I was searching for the meaning of life, but also because I was inventing and refining my view of the world, my ethical sensibility, using the insights I gleaned from the novels of such masters as Tolstoy, Stendhal, Proust, Mann, Dostoyevsky, and Woolf.

Some novelists, who are aware of the fact that the center of the novel emerges gradually during the process of composition, begin writing their novels without much planning. They decide what is superfluous and what is missing, what is too short and what is too long, which character is superficial and which is unnecessary, as they discover and perfect the center; and they craft the details when they revise. Sometimes they write thousands of pages but cannot decide on the center. They may die before determining the overall shape of their novel, leaving this task up to eager editors or scholars.

Other novelists decide on the center of the novel from the outset, and try to proceed without making any concessions whatsoever. This method is much more difficult than writing a novel without careful planning or taking the center into consideration, and especially so during the writing of the opening sections. Tolstoy expended great effort on *War and Peace,* changing and rewriting pages time and time again. But the truly intriguing aspect of this effort was that the center, the main idea of the novel, remained the same throughout the entire four years he took to write the book. At the end of *War and Peace,* Tolstoy added an essay discussing the role of the individual in history—a piece of such length and earnestness that we immediately realize he wants us to believe this is the spirit, the subject, the goal, and the center of the novel. But for today's readers, the center and main idea of *War and Peace* is not the subject Tolstoy discusses at the end of the novel—the point of history and the role of the individual in history—but the intense and compassionate attention the characters give to the details of everyday life, and the clear, all-encompassing gaze that unites the various life stories in the novel. When we've finished reading the book, what remains in our mind is not history and its meaning, but our thoughts on the fragility of human life, the immensity of the world, and our place in the universe; and in the course of reading, we have had the pleasure of experiencing the sentence-by-sentence illumination of a center. So one might conclude that the center of a novel relies on the pleasures we derive from the text as much as it does on the writer's intent.

Describing this center—which changes according to the writer's intentions, the text's implications, the reader's tastes, and the time and place in which the novel is read—may seem as impossible as the attempt to identify the center of the world or the meaning of life. But this is exactly what I will try to do now.

The challenge of defining the center of a literary novel should remind us that the literary novel is an entity whose meaning is difficult to articulate or to reduce to anything else—just like the meaning of life. The modern secular individual, despite recognizing deep down the futility of his effort, cannot help reflecting on the meaning of life as he tries to locate the center of the novel he is reading—for in seeking this center, he is seeking the center of his own life and that of the world. If we are reading a literary novel, a work whose center is not obvious, one of our main motivations is the need to reflect on that center and determine how close it is to our own view of existence.

The center sometimes lies within the great panorama itself, in the beauty and clarity of the narrative details, as it does in *War and Peace.* At other times, it is closely related to the technique and form of the novel, as it is in *Ulysses.* In *Ulysses,* the center is not about the plot, the themes, or even the subject; it consists in the pleasure of poetically revealing the workings of the human mind and, in the process, describing and illuminating aspects of our life that had previously been neglected. But once a writer of Joyce's caliber has wrought such an essential change in the novel via particular techniques and their effects, the same invention will never again have the same power for the reader. Faulkner, among others, learned a great deal from Joyce, yet the most powerful aspect of *The Sound and the Fury* and *As I Lay Dying,* his most brilliant novels, is no longer a marvelous display of the characters' thinking and the inside of their minds. We are impressed, instead, by the way in which their inner monologues are knit together, giving us a fresh vision of the world and of life. Faulkner learned from Conrad how to play with narrative voice and how to tell a story by moving backward and forward in time. Virginia Woolf's novel *The Waves* uses the same impressionist technique of juxtaposition. *Mrs.*

Dalloway, by contrast, reveals how our small, ordinary thoughts—as well as our more dramatic feelings, regret and pride, and the objects that surround us—interweave and overlap at each passing moment. But the first writer who fanatically pursued the idea of composing a novel from the restricted point of view of a single character was Henry James. There were, said James in a letter to Mrs. Humphry Ward (July 25, 1899), "five million ways" to tell a story, and each one could be justified if it provided a "center" for the work.

Speaking of this chain of influences, I would like to remind you that novels also reveal their depth of meaning via the forms and techniques they employ—for every new way of telling a story or constructing a novel means looking at life through a new window.

In the course of my life as a novelist, I have read the novels of other writers—hopefully, eagerly, sometimes despairingly—casting about for a new viewpoint and wondering if those novels might help me find it. Every perfect window through which I wanted to survey the world and which I pictured in my mind's eye would have a small and invented personal history attached.

Here is an example of a personal history to help me clarify what I am referring to as the center. I just mentioned Faulkner. (John Updike wrote somewhere that he could not understand why all Third World writers were so influenced by Faulkner.) Faulkner's novel *The Wild Palms* is actually composed of a pair of stories, which the writer said in an interview had originally been separate and distinct works. In combining them, Faulkner did not closely interweave the stories, but merely layered the chapters of the two tales as though he were shuffling two decks of cards. In the book, we first read part of a love story, fraught with difficulties, involving a pair of lovers named Henry and Charlotte. Then we read the first chapter of another story entitled "Old Man," which tells of a convict struggling against floods in Mississippi. Nowhere in *The Wild Palms* do the two stories intersect; in fact, some publishers have actually issued "Old Man" as a novel in itself. But since they are parts of the novel called *The Wild Palms,* we read them by comparing them, seeking their common points, and, yes, by looking for their shared center. Considering one or the other story individually—say, "Old Man"—we attribute different meanings to it when we read it as a separate book and when we read it as a part of the novel *The Wild Palms.* This fact reminds us that a novel is defined by its center. The difference between the *Arabian Nights* (the *Thousand and One Nights*) and *In Search of Lost Time* is that the latter has a center we are very aware of, and that we read its various parts—which are sometimes published, just like

the tales within the *Arabian Nights,* as separate novels
(e.g., *Swann in Love*)—by constantly searching for this
center.

When analyzing the evolution of the novel as a genre,
literary critics and historians have devoted little attention to the center, in their studies of fiction and
fictionality and in their admiring histories of the concepts of time and representation. One reason for this is
that the center in the nineteenth-century novel does
not manifest itself clearly as a force sustaining the
novel and binding together its parts; so there appears
to be little need for a real or imaginary focal point for
the narrative threads. The integrating factor in the
nineteenth-century novel is sometimes a disaster like
the plague (as in *The Betrothed,* by Alessandro Man-
zoni), sometimes war (as in Tolstoy's *War and Peace*),
and sometimes a literary character who lends his or
her name to the book. Often, fateful coincidences (as in
the works of Eugène Sue) or chance meetings on city
streets (as in Victor Hugo's *Les Misérables*) serve to jos-
tle the characters together and connect the parts of the
novel's landscape. It is rather surprising that literary
criticism has been reluctant to explore the notion of
the center, even after the elements that I have been calling the "landscape" of the novel were clearly identified,
and even after novelists such as Faulkner, in the twen-

tieth century, developed narrative techniques of dispersion, fragmentation, and cut-and-paste. Another reason for this reserve may be that deconstructionist theory spurns overly simplistic binary oppositions in literary texts—dichotomies such as interior-exterior, appearance-essence, matter-mind, good-evil.

After *The Wild Palms* was translated into Spanish by Borges, it influenced an entire generation of Latin American writers. A series of brilliant, semi-Dadaist novels followed in the footsteps of *The Wild Palms,* and transformed the pleasure of reading into the quest for a center. Here is a personal list: Vladimir Nabokov's *Pale Fire* (1962), Julio Cortázar's *Hopscotch* (1963), Guillermo Cabrera Infante's *Three Trapped Tigers* (1967), V. S. Naipaul's *In a Free State* (1971), Italo Calvino's *Invisible Cities* (1973) and *If on a Winter's Night a Traveler* (1979), Mario Vargas-Llosa's *Aunt Julia and the Scriptwriter* (1977), Georges Perec's *Life: A User's Manual* (1978), Milan Kundera's *Unbearable Lightness of Being* (1984), and Julian Barnes's *History of the World in 10½ Chapters* (1989). These novels, all of which were received with great interest and immediately translated into many languages, reminded readers worldwide and budding novelists like me of something that had been known since Rabelais and Sterne—namely, that anything and everything could be included in a novel: lists and inventories, melodramatic radio plays, strange poems and poetic commentaries, the mixed-up parts of various novels, essays on history and science, philosophical texts, encyclopedic trivia, historical tales, digressions and anecdotes, and anything else that might come to mind. People were now reading novels not primarily to understand characters at odds with the realities of their world, or to see how their habits and personal traits were illuminated by the plot, but to think directly about the structure of life.

Mikhail Bakhtin's studies of the polyphonic novel and his revaluations of Rabelais and Sterne, as well as the rediscovery of the eighteenth-century novel and the works of Diderot, legitimized this great change in the landscape of the nineteenth-century novel. Reading each of those novels, I searched for a center, as Borges did when reading *Moby-Dick;* and I understood that digressions and detours from the supposed subject, in the style of *Tristram Shandy,* were actually the real subject of the work.

In my novel *The Black Book,* a character describes the work of newspaper columnists in terms that apply equally to the process of composing a novel: novel-writing, for me, is the art of talking about important things as if they were irrelevant, and about unimportant things as if they were relevant. Anyone who reads a novel that has been written with complete fidelity to this principle will have to search for and imagine the center in every sentence and every paragraph, in order to understand what is important and what is not. If we are, as Schiller says, sentimental (rather than naive) novelists—in other words, overtly aware of our narrative methods—we know that the reader will try to imagine the center of our novel by taking the text's form into consideration. I believe that the highest achievement of a novelist, as a creator and an artist, is the ability to construct the form of a novel as an enigma—a puzzle whose solution reveals the novel's center. Perhaps even the most naive reader will realize, when reading such a novel, that the key to the meaning, to the center, lies in solving this enigma. In the literary novel, the enigma is not about guessing the murderer, but about working out just what the true subject of the novel is, just as Borges did when reading *Moby-Dick*. When a novel reaches this level of complexity and subtlety, the form of the narrative, not its subject, becomes the matter of greatest curiosity.

Calvino wrote a polemical article in the 1970s—the decade during which he composed the two novels I mentioned above—in which he foresaw the consequences of this situation. The essay, entitled "The Novel as Spectacle," described the changes that were taking place in the art of the novel around that time: "The novel, or what in experimental literature has taken the place of the novel, has as its very first rule not to rely on a story (or a world) outside its own pages. The reader is called upon only to follow the process of writing, the text in the act of being written." This means that the reader will take the form of the novel to be the overall view, which remains obscured by individual trees so long as he is immersed in the landscape; and he will search for the center in a location corresponding to it.

The best example of the novelist who completely distances himself from the naive state of mind, and becomes "sentimental" in Schiller's sense, is the novelist who strives to see and read his own novel from the viewpoint of the reader. This approach, as Horace said, resembles the act of gazing repeatedly at a landscape painting we have made—stepping back slightly to gain a new perspective, moving closer, stepping back again. But we have to pretend that the person looking at the painting is someone else. Then we remember that what we call the center is actually a construct of our own making. To write a novel is to create a center we cannot find in life or in the world, and to hide it within the landscape—playing an imaginary game of chess with our audience.

To read a novel is to perform the same gesture in reverse. The only thing the writer and the reader place between them is the text of the novel, as if it were an entertaining sort of chessboard. Every reader visualizes the text in his own way, and seeks the center wherever he likes.

Still, we know that this is not a random game. The manners our parents taught us, the public or private schooling we had, the precepts of religion, myth, and custom, the paintings we admire, the novels we have read, both good and bad, even the puzzles in children's magazines that invite us to "find the path that leads to the rabbit hole at the center of the labyrinth"—all have taught us that there is a center, and have suggested where and how we might search for it. The acts of writing and reading novels are carried out in harmony with this education, as well as in reaction against it.

The fact that there is no single center became apparent to me when I read literary novels and when I saw the world through the eyes of characters who clashed with one another. The Cartesian world in which mind and matter, human figures and landscapes, logic and imagination are separate and distinct cannot be the world of the novel. It can only be the world of a power, an authority, that wants to control everything—for instance, the single-centered world of the modern nation-state. More than the passing of an overall judgment on an entire landscape, the task of reading a novel is the joy of experiencing every obscure corner, every person, every color and shade of the landscape. When we read a novel, we devote our primary energy not to judging the entire text or to logically comprehending it, but to transforming it into pictures, clear and detailed in our imagination, and to taking our place within this gallery of images, opening our senses to all its many stimuli. Thus, the hope of finding a center encourages us to be mentally and sensually receptive, to employ our imagination with hope and optimism, to enter the novel quickly, and to locate ourselves within the story.

I do not refer to hope and optimism lightly: the act of reading a novel is the effort to believe that the world actually does have a center, and this takes all the confidence one can muster. The great literary novels—such as *Anna Karenina, In Search of Lost Time, The Magic Mountain,* and *The Waves*—are indispensable to us because they create the hope and the vivid illusion that the world has a center and a meaning, and because they give us joy by sustaining this impression as we turn their pages. (This knowledge of life, which *The Magic Mountain* imparts, is ultimately a far more compelling prize than the stolen diamond in a detective novel.) We want to reread such novels once we finish them—not because we have located the center, but because we want to experience once again this feeling of optimism. Our effort to identify with and acknowledge one by one all the characters and their viewpoints, the energy we expend when transforming words into images, and myriad other actions we rapidly and carefully perform in our mind while we read a great novel—all these create within us the feeling that novels have more than one center. We learn this not through leisurely thought or abstruse concepts, but through the experience of reading. For the modern secular individual, one way to find a deeper, more profound meaning in the world is to read the great literary novels. When we read them, we understand that not only the world but also our own mind has more than one center.

In saying this, I am referring to the many different actions we perform when reading a novel: our effort to understand characters with disparate attitudes and morals, our ability to believe simultaneously in contradictory views, our move to identify with those different views without being unsettled, just as if they were our own. While reading literary novels with ambiguous centers, and searching for a center, we also sense that our mind has the capacity to believe in many things at once—and that neither our mind nor the world actually contains a center. The dilemma here is between our need for a center in order to understand, and our urge to resist the power of this center and its dominant logic. We know from our own experience that the desire to understand the world has a political aspect; and the same is true of our instinct to resist the center. A genuine response to such dilemmas can be found only through literary novels that present a unique balance between clarity and ambiguity, control and interpretive freedom, composition and fragmentation. *Murder on the Orient Express* (because its center is too obvious) and *Finnegans Wake* (because for a reader like me, there is almost no hope of finding in it a center or any kind of accessible meaning) are not novels of this type. The audience that a novel addresses, when and how it speaks, and the subjects it deals with—all of this changes over time. As does the center of the novel.

I have mentioned the excitement that Dostoyevsky felt, while writing *The Devils*, when a new center emerged from within the story. All novelists know this feeling: in the process of writing, we suddenly have new ideas about the deeper reaches and meaning of our book, about what it will imply when it is finished. Then we review and reconsider what we have already written, in the light of this new center. For me, the task of writing entails gradually maneuvering the center into place by adding new passages, scenes, and details, finding new characters, identifying with them, removing and

adding voices, composing new situations and dialogues while getting rid of others, and adding many
things that I had not imagined when I began. I read
somewhere that Tolstoy, in one of his conversations,
suggested a very simple professional formula: "If the
hero of a novel is too evil, one must add a little good-
ness, and if he is too good, one must add a little evil." I
would like to make a similar comment, in the same naive vein: if I realize that the center is too obvious, I hide
it, and if the center is too obscure, I feel I must reveal it
a little.

The power of a novel's center ultimately resides not
in what it is, but in our search for it as readers. Reading
a novel of fine balance and detail, we never discover a
center in any definite sense—yet we never completely
abandon the hope of finding it. Both the center and the
meaning of the novel change from one reader to the
next. When we discuss the nature of the center—which
Borges called the subject—we are discussing our view
of life. These are the points of tension that keep us
reading novels, and our curiosity is sustained by these
questions. As we move through the landscape of the
novel, and as we read other literary novels, we come to
feel the center vividly by believing in and by identifying
with contradictory voices, thoughts, and states of mind.
This whole effort keeps the reader from making hasty

moral judgments about the characters and about the writer.

Our suspension of moral judgment enables us to understand novels most deeply. My wording here is intended to evoke Coleridge's famous remark about the "willing suspension of disbelief." Coleridge coined this phrase in order to explain how fantastic literature was made possible. In the two centuries that have passed since he published his *Biographia Literaria* in 1817, the art of the novel, along with the establishment and consolidation of what I am calling the center, has marginalized poetry and other literary genres to become the world's dominant literary form. Novelists have accomplished this, over the course of two centuries, by searching for that strange and profound thing, the center, in the ordinary, everyday details of life and by reorganizing them.

In the same passage of the *Biographia Literaria*, Coleridge reminds us that his friend Wordsworth strove to achieve a different effect in poetry. Here, according to Coleridge, is Wordsworth's goal: "To give charm of novelty to things of every day, and to excite a feeling analogous to the supernatural, by awakening the mind's attention from the lethargy of custom, and directing it to the loveliness and wonders of the world before us." In my thirty-five years as a novelist, this is what I have always thought Tolstoy did, as well as Dostoyevsky, Proust, and Mann—the great novelists who have taught me the art of the novel.

I think that, far from being a coincidence, it was an invocation of the basic dilemmas of the art of the novel that prompted Tolstoy to place Anna on the St. Petersburg train with a novel in her hands and a window giving onto a landscape which reflected her mood. What kind of novel would Anna have to be holding—what kind of narrative would seize her imagination so powerfully—that she would be unable to lift her eyes from the page? We can never know. But in order for us to enter the landscape that Tolstoy had inhabited, known, and explored—and in order for him to place us in it with her—Anna had to look not at the book, but through the window of the train. With Anna's gaze, a whole landscape comes to life before our eyes. We must thank Anna, for we enter the novel through this gaze—her gaze—and find ourselves in the Russia of the 1870s. Because Anna Karenina could not read the novel she held in her hands, we read *Anna Karenina* the novel.

Epilogue

In the fall of 2008, Homi Bhabha phoned me from Cambridge and kindly asked whether I would deliver the Norton Lectures at Harvard University. Ten days later, we met for lunch in New York to discuss the details. The general idea for this book, though not the specific chapters, had already taken shape in my mind. I knew what my feelings and motivations were, and what I wanted to accomplish in the book.

As to my feelings and motivations: Shortly before the meeting in New York, I had completed *The Museum of Innocence*, the novel that had taken ten years of planning and four years of writing. It had been published in Istanbul, and I was happy that the book was being so well received by Turkish readers, in the wake of a great deal of political unrest. *The Museum of Innocence* seemed like a return to the fictional and personal world of my first novel, *Cevdet Bey and Sons*. It resembled the earlier book not only in its setting and plot, but also in its form—that of the traditional nineteenth-century novel. I felt as if my thirty-five-year journey as a novelist had, after numerous adventures and a series of fascinating way-stations, made a giant circle, bringing me back to my original starting point.

But as we all know, the place we return to is never the same place we left. In this sense, it was as if my novel-writing had traced not a circle, but the initial loop of a spiral. My mind held an image of the literary journey I had been on, and I was ready and willing to talk about it, like someone who had returned from a long voyage and was joyously preparing for another.

As to my goals for the book: I wanted to talk about my novelistic journey, the stops I'd made along the way, what the art and form of the novel had taught me, the limits they had imposed upon me, my struggles with and attachment to them. At the same time, I wanted my lectures to be an essay or meditation on the art of the novel, rather than a trip down memory lane or a discussion of my personal development. This book is an integral whole comprising all the most important things I know and have learned about the novel. As is apparent from its size, this is of course not a history of the novel—although in my efforts to understand the art of the novel, I do occasionally refer to the evolution of the genre. But my main goal has been to explore the effects that novels have on their readers, how novelists work, and how novels are written. My experiences as a novel-reader and novel-writer are intertwined. The best way to study the novel is to read the great novels and aspire to write something like them. At times, I feel the truth in Nietzsche's words: before speaking of art, one must try to create a work of art.

Compared to other novelists I know, I see myself as someone who is more interested in theory and who enjoys reading about theories of the novel—an interest that proved useful when, after the age of fifty, I started teaching at Columbia University. This book, however, was written to express my views on the subject, not to explore conceptual points or to engage with other theories.

My worldview aligns closely with my current understanding of the novel. When, at twenty-two, I declared to my family, friends, and acquaintances, "I am not going to be a painter—I am going to be a novelist!" and began in earnest to write my first novel, everyone warned me, perhaps to protect me from a bleak future (that of devoting a lifetime to writing novels in a country with a small readership): "Orhan, nobody understands life at twenty-two! Wait until you get older and know something about life, people, and the world— then you can write your novel." (They thought I wanted to write just one novel.) I was furious at these words, and wanted everyone to hear my reply: We write novels not because we feel we understand life and people, but because we feel we understand other novels and the art of the novel, and wish to write in a similar way.

Now, thirty-five years later, I feel more sympathetic toward the views of my well-intentioned acquaintances. For the past ten years I have been writing novels in order to convey the way I see life, the world, the things I have encountered, and the place where I live. In this book, too, I have given priority to my own experiences, but in many places I have described my point of view via well-known texts and observations by others.

My comments here are not restricted to the stage I have now reached in my thinking. In these lectures, I speak not only about the thoughts I had on the art of the novel while writing *The Museum of Innocence,* but also about the experience and knowledge I gained from all of my previous novels.

Cevdet Bey and Sons, which I started to write in 1974, conservatively followed the template of nineteenth-century realist novels such as *Buddenbrooks* or *Anna Karenina.* Later on, with a definite sense of excitement, I forced myself to be modernist and experimental. *The Silent House,* my second novel, shows influences ranging from Faulkner to Woolf, from the French *nouveau roman* to the Latin American novel. (Unlike Nabokov, who denied being influenced by other writers, I believe that speaking with a certain amount of exaggeration about such influences is both liberating and, as in this context, instructive.) To use an old expression, I "found my own voice" by opening myself up to writers like Borges and Calvino. The first example of this is my historical novel *The White Castle*. In the book you are reading now, I have talked about such writers in the light of my experiences. *The Black Book* is autobiographical, like my first novel, but at the same time it is quite different, for it is the first novel in which I discovered my true inner voice. It must have been during the writing of *The Black Book* that I started forming the theory of plot I discuss here. Likewise, I developed my ideas on the visual aspects of narration while writing *My Name Is Red*. In all of my novels, I have tried to mobilize the reader's visual imagination and have adhered to my belief that the art of the novel works— despite the striking counterexample of Dostoyevsky— through visuality. *Snow* led me to think about the conjunction of the novel and politics, while *The Museum of Innocence* developed my ideas on the representation of social reality. When novelists embark on a new book, we draw on the accumulated experience of all our previous novels, and the knowledge gained from all those earlier volumes helps and supports us. But we are also entirely alone, just as we were when we wrote the opening sentence of our very first novel.

In October 2009, on my way to meet Homi Bhabha in New York, I was thinking of two books that could serve as models for these lectures. The first was E. M. Forster's *Aspects of the Novel,* a book I was convinced was outdated. It had been dropped from the syllabus in university English departments and exiled to creative-writing programs, where writing is treated as a craft and not as a spiritual and philosophical act. But after rereading Forster's book, I felt that its reputation should be restored. The other book I had in mind was *The Theory of the Novel,* written by the Hungarian critic-philosopher György Lukács in the period before he became a Marxist. Rather than a detailed theory of the novel, his book is more of a philosophical, anthropological, surprisingly poetic essay that tries to figure out why humanity has a spiritual need for a mirror (a custom-built mirror!) such as the novel. I have always wanted to write a book that, while speaking about the art of the novel, engaged in a profound discussion about all humanity, especially the modern individual.

The first great writer who realized that he could discuss all humanity while talking about himself was, of course, Montaigne. Thanks to his method—and to many others developed in the modern novel, starting with the point-of-view technique conceived in the early twentieth century—we novelists have, I think, finally understood that our primary task is to identify with our characters. In this book, I have drawn strength from a Montaigne-like optimism: an optimism based on the belief that if I frankly discuss my own experience of writing novels, and what I do when I write and read novels, then I will be discussing all novelists and the art of the novel in general.

But just as there are limits on our ability to identify with characters unlike ourselves, and on the extent to which our autobiographical characters can represent all humanity, I know there is a limit on my optimism as an essayist—a writer of nonfiction. When Forster and Lukács spoke about the art of the novel, they did not emphasize the fact that their views were early twentieth-century Eurocentric views, because a hundred years ago the art of the novel, as everyone knew, was exclusively a European, or Western, art. Nowadays, the genre of the novel is used all over the globe. The remarkable way it has spread is a constant topic of discussion. Over the past one hundred fifty years, the novel has marginalized traditional literary forms in every country where it has appeared, becoming the dominant form, in a process paralleling the establishment of nation-states. Now, in every corner of the world, the vast majority of those who want to express themselves through literature write novels. Two years ago, my publishers in Shanghai told me that young writers were sending them tens of thousands of manuscripts every year—so many that it was impossible to read them all. I believe this is the case all over the world. Communication through literature, in or outside the West, is predominantly carried out via the novel. Perhaps this is why contemporary novelists sense that their stories and characters are limited in their ability to represent the whole of humanity.

Likewise, I am aware that my experience as a novelist enables me to speak only partially for all novelists. I hope the reader will keep in mind that this book was written from the point of view of a self-taught writer who came of age in 1970s Turkey, a culture with a fairly weak tradition of writing novels and reading books, and who decided to become a novelist by reading the books in his father's library and whatever else he could find, essentially fumbling around in the dark. Yet I also believe that my comments on the way we visualize and transform words in our imagination do not spring solely from my love for painting. I believe that they highlight a basic feature of the art of the novel.

When I was in my twenties and first read the essay by Schiller that informs this book, I wanted to become a naive writer. Back then, in the 1970s, the most popular and influential Turkish novelists wrote semi-political,

semi-poetic novels that took place in rural settings and
small villages. In those days, becoming a naive writer
whose stories were set in the city, in Istanbul, seemed a
difficult goal to achieve. Since I delivered these lectures at Harvard, I have been asked repeatedly, "Mr.
Pamuk, are you a naive novelist or a sentimental one?"
I would like to emphasize that, for me, the ideal state
is one in which the novelist is naive and sentimental at
the same time.

In late 2008, at Columbia University's Butler Library,
I did a great deal of reading on fictional character and
the theory of plot. I then wrote the major part of these
lectures, relying on what I remembered from other
books and sources. In 2009, after air flights in Rajas-
than were canceled as a result of the global economic
crisis, I traveled with Kiran Desai in a hired car across
the golden-hued desert between Jaisalmer and Jodh-
pur. On the way, amid the heat of the desert, I reread
Schiller's essay and was filled with the vision—almost a
mirage—of writing this book. I wrote these lectures in
Goa, in Istanbul, in Venice (while I was teaching at Ca'
Foscari University), in Greece (in a rented house across
from the island of Spetses), and in New York. They assumed their final form in Widener Library at Harvard
University, and in Stephen Greenblatt's book-filled
home in Cambridge. Compared with my novels, this

book took shape quite easily—perhaps because I decided to maintain a conversational tone. Often, I would take out my notebook in airports, hotels, and cafés (most memorably at the Métropole, a café in Flaubert's Rouen where Sartre and Beauvoir used to meet in the 1930s), and would immerse myself in the subject, effortlessly and happily adding a few paragraphs in the space of an hour. The only challenge I faced was the requirement that each lecture take no more than about fifty minutes. When I write a novel, if I come up with ideas and details that enrich the text, I can always extend the chapter. But the time limit imposed on the lectures forced me to become my own most ruthless critic and editor.

I would like to express my thanks to Nazim Dikbaş, my friend and translator; to Kiran Desai, who subsequently read this English translation and provided invaluable advice; to David Damrosch, who has read all the books in the world and whose countless suggestions strengthened the argument; and to Homi Bhabha, whose warm hospitality made me feel at home in Cambridge.

Index